Making It Make Sense

Memoir

Table of Contents

Dedication

I want to dedicate this book to the people that never left my side, supported me, and believed in me. And to my dogs that remained and still remain by my side.

And last but not least...

"I want to thank me for doing all this hard work, I want to thank me for having no days off, I want to thank me for never quitting, I want to thank me for always being a giver and trying to give more than I receive." -Snoop Dogg

For Entertainment Purposes Only

I used to feel safe

I could cry alone

Now I hold it in

Until it has to be shown

You stole my life

It wasn't right

How could you do this to me

I was happy

My privacy has been taken

My walls are now down

I have nothing left

At least what wasn't kept

I am more than what you thought

There's things you never caught

I guess you forgot

Who I am

You can't always watch

And think you know

There's some things that just won't show

I'm more than what you did

I have more to give

You couldn't steal that see

I chose to live

I am not a victim

I just don't know how to pick 'em

One day I'll be

With someone who'll see

What I let them

I hope one day

You'll feel like me

More than what's happened to you

A person that's free

You can't steal a person

No matter how hard you try

I'll rebuild myself

While I cry

I'm stronger than you thought

You think you won't get caught

Lmao

Mic Drop

The Beginning

The beginning of the end... or so I thought. Well, let me explain. Hi. I'm Brooke, and I'm a victim. I'm a victim of identity theft, gaslighting, and more to be determined. I'd used the saying, always wear shoes when walking through BS. It was a nod to my broken toes and the BS that followed.

On June 25, 2021, I received an email from our cell phone carrier, "my husband's cell phone account," with an updated order status. We'd just purchased a cellphone for my youngest stepdaughter on June 21, 2021, but we had already received it. At first, I thought it was concerning her phone. The email was odd because why would I be getting the email and not my husband? My email was never on that account. And why an order status update on something received?

I immediately called the company to question this and was told no worries; this is a normal promotional email that goes out. Huh? That's about all I thought. I filed this incident away in my brain in what I like to call my "wtf" folder. You know, it's there when needed, but not before.

I'd recently started a new position within the company I worked for and was having trouble with my work-issued laptop that I had waited two weeks to receive. Nothing worked. I spent every morning on the phone with our IT department for at least forty-five minutes. I was not transitioning well since starting my new job on June 1, 2021, due to that and also my coworkers.

I wasn't new to the company. I'd been there eleven years. I just changed departments and was no longer working shift work. My coworkers were people I'd known the entire time. One lady I had worked with and trained personally, yet despite this, on my first day, no one spoke to me. At all. I walked in excited and ready to learn something new! It felt good not to have to be at work so early anymore. I had plenty of sleep the night before, and once inside the office, I said, "Good morning, ladies," and no one even looked at me.

I was treated that way pretty much every day after that. If someone did speak to me, it wasn't exactly friendly. I felt out of place and they made sure of it. It was the first time in my life I felt as if I didn't fit in. The first time I'd been purposely excluded.

I was not adjusting well because of the hostile environment I now found myself in. During this time in my life, everything was getting filed in the wtf folder. I didn't have time for it. I needed to focus at work and learn my new job. No one trained me. I was constantly being questioned as to why I was so behind on my work, but also being told to help my coworkers with their work load. I'd received some training on their jobs, but my job required more than the two hours spent.

I went from being the senior person in my previous job and someone that people would come to for help to the new girl who needed help all the time. It was hard for me, and I'd not anticipated this feeling.

One thing about me, though, and I've ALWAYS been this way; if it doesn't make sense, I can't let it go. Hence the folder. So I noted everything. Literally. I started writing everything that was happening in a notebook.

A few days later, I started noticing weird things on my cell phone. My Memojis were unicorns. Unicorns y'all. Not me. Not ever. I'm just not a unicorn fan. No offense.

My life was starting to shift. Everything I was used to was gone and I was in unknown territory and I didn't like it. I had no idea just how much it was going to change, but for me, getting the new job was the beginning of the end.

Unicorns

Unicorns on my phone. Yep. That's how it started. One day, I was minding my business, doing what I do, working, coming home, being with my family, and hanging out with friends. Then I started noticing unicorns on my phone.

When you go into your phone to send a text message, there's always a frequently used option for your emojis. Well, I don't like unicorns, but yet there they were, nine of them. Frequently used, and just as soon as I noticed them, they were gone. So every time I'd try to go show someone what was going on with my phone, I looked crazy because they'd disappear. That was the first red flag.

About a week later, July 9, 2021, to be exact, my phone began acting up to the point where it was barely usable. I couldn't send emails. I couldn't make phone calls. I couldn't send text messages. I had a suspicion that things were off with my stepdaughters and their devices.

I noticed that every time they were at our home, things would get worse for me on my devices. We often checked our step-daughter's phones because they were underage and we wanted to make sure that they weren't doing anything that they shouldn't be. When we went through the oldest daughter's phone, I noticed that she had several messages between her and her mom with Apple ID verification codes. That's odd because what would be the reason for this? The codes allow for another device to sign into your iCloud account.

Now, my stepdaughters were signed into our Apple iCloud Family account. See, what they don't tell you at Apple is if you have a shared iCloud account, it's not just about sharing your music. The way it was put to me is that it's kind of like a storage unit where everyone stores all of their boxes in one unit, and you have to walk past other people's boxes to get to your own. So the ability to see all of my information was always there. You just have to know how to do it. Do I think that my underage stepdaughters knew how to do that? No. Do I think that their mom knew how? Absolutely. She had already shown how unethical she was over the years. I brought this to the attention of Apple to see if they could verify what I was seeing.

They also saw it, except they couldn't fix it. They told me that because it was a person doing this to me. I was screwed. There was no coming back from this. You will not recover. Short of changing your name and your social security number, you will not recover. You need to move out of your home and away from these people, is what they said. They referred to it as "the perfect storm." Anything that could go wrong had.

I was happy. I loved my family. I didn't want to move. I didn't want to change my name. Why me? Why would I have to go through this? On the evening of July 9th, 2021, and the morning of July 10th, 2021, I discovered all of the Apple verification codes on my stepdaughter's phone via text messages with her mother.

She would receive a code and screenshot it and send it to her mother so her mother could access the iCloud account. According to the messages I was to see, this had been going on for quite some time. The girls both got new cellphones from their mom at Christmas in 2020. So it started immediately on the phones we were looking at. I imagine it was already going on even prior to Christmas.

My husband gifted me a brand-new MacBook for Christmas, and I was so excited! I'd always wanted one. I only used my MacBook for important things like filing taxes or signing mortgage papers. They're supposed to be safe and the least likely to get a virus or hacked, I thought.

We had an Amazon Echo Dot with the Alexa feature in our bathroom. Yes, I know. Everyone's probably wondering, "Why did she have an Alexa in her bathroom?" But you see, my husband used it as a speaker so that he could listen to music while he was in the shower and I never thought anything of it. You can have conversations on there if you want as well. Cool, huh?

Well, one of the features of Alexa is called a drop-in feature, where if someone has your login information or you give them permission, they have the ability to drop in on your Alexa and listen to anything that's going on. We had two in our home. We had one in our main living area and one in our master bathroom.

That afternoon, while I was in the bathroom, I heard the ex-wife talking to her other daughter by her current husband, and I thought to myself, "Great. Now she's in my head. I've completely lost my mind. I'm hearing voices," and I'm having this conversation with myself knowing that this is the moment. That's it. I've lost it. I've lost it completely. I've had a nervous breakdown. This is what it feels like, and then something caught my eye. Well, another feature that Alexa offers is when someone's dropping in, it lights up green and spins around.

Quietly, I walked over to Alexa to listen to make sure that was what I had heard. Sure enough, it was her talking to her other daughter. I'm assuming she forgot to hit the mute button. I quickly ran outside to get my husband so that he could witness this. He also heard it. He unplugged the Alexa. I immediately contacted Amazon once I was able to make a phone call. I wanted the analytic report. I wanted proof that this happened, where it was coming from, and then it hit me!

This probably wasn't the first time! We've had Alexa for four years at this point. How long had this been going on and how many accounts were hacked? Because now I know it's all of my devices. I always thought it was odd that the girls would tell me things that their mom said about my husband and me. For example, one day, shortly before this situation, they said their mom told them my husband and I fight all of the time. Well, that's not true, but I remember saying to them, how would she know if we were? And I noted that conversation because of how odd it was.

What in the world was going on? Now she's listening in?! Been listening in?! The ex-wife had already been to our home that Saturday morning at 8:30 to retrieve the girls' devices. She somehow knew immediately we'd been hacked. How could she know? I wasn't able to call or text anyone, and my husband said it was all of our phones, but somehow she knew. She never came to our home. He always went to her and yet here she was at our home, out of her vehicle and at the front door.

When I say at our front door, I actually mean she was leaning on it. One foot inside my home and one foot out. It was weird! I took note of this because it reminded me of a dog trying to mark its territory. I was extremely uneasy. It was as if she was letting me know she could do whatever she wanted. And well, if I'm being honest, she could.

While standing halfway inside my home, uninvited, talking to both girls, the oldest says, we've been hacked and have to go to the AT&T store. Are you coming with us? She says this to her mom and the youngest says, wait, why would she be coming? Her mother nor the oldest answered her.

I stood in my bedroom listening to this conversation and I thought the same thing. Why would she be coming? That's weird. It was all I could do not to confront her and cause a scene, but over the last ten years, my husband always had her back and not mine and honestly, I didn't want to upset him. That was all that was said and she left with the devices.

I called Apple again after many resets on my phone. Apple and I were on a first-name basis at this point. They advised me to pull my Google Gmail analytic report. It's free. If you haven't done that, you should because Google will provide you with any email address and password that has ever used your email address for an alias. For example, you can create a Microsoft family account from my email address if you know my password, which you would if you had access to my devices.

When I pulled my Google Analytics report, it provided me with those email addresses and the passwords to those accounts. I was provided with three email addresses. Two belonged to my husband's ex-wife, and one belonged to my stepdaughter. I decided to go into my stepdaughter's email. She had two folders, one with all of her drawings and writings. She likes to write stories, and the other folder was all of my personal information that came off of my Apple MacBook. W-2s, driver's license, social security card, pay stubs, everything right there.

You can imagine how upset I was. Or can you? How does one feel when that happens to them? It's crazy, right? Because why would someone do that? What would be the purpose? Apple told me that anyone that has AirPods or a watch, anything with Bluetooth capability that is their product, has the ability to steal all of your information off of your device if your Bluetooth is on as well. So not only did she have access through iCloud, she could just retrieve the files via Bluetooth, and with email access as well, she could intercept email notifications I would receive when a new account like the Microsoft account was created. A perfect storm.

AT&T, my service provider at that time, was of no help. We even paid for fraud detection as an add-on to our plan. They had no explanation for it. My name had been removed as an authorized user from the account and changed to my previous last name to another phone number. They couldn't tell me when this occurred or who did it.

On their website, they teach you about SIM jacking and mirroring devices, which is what Apple said also was happening to me as well. I don't know who knows this, but I did not know that this was a capability because I'm not a hacker.

Apple and the phone companies teach you how to do it. It's Hacker 101. The ability is there. You just have to have some type of ethics. They used that ability to mirror my device to other devices. Everything I emailed, everything I texted, anything that was in writing, any files, pictures, all of that information could be seen in live time when it happened. What we didn't know was if I had a conversation on the phone, could that be heard? We weren't sure of that.

That would need an outside recording device, they thought, but they weren't sure. At this point, I decided to quit talking. If I didn't say anything, then no one could know anything, right? I stopped talking and I started sitting outside because I couldn't sit in my home anymore. I didn't feel safe.

I ended up going to the police station to file a police report, not thinking that they would do anything about it. I just wanted a police report as a formality so that I could take this information to the bank to my financial institutions, which were also hacked. Every single account that I owned from A to Z, whether it was a shopping account, a financial account, or a car insurance account, every single thing had been hacked. A few days later, the police decided that they would actually look into this. The detectives called me in.

I brought in my devices voluntarily with my proof of where it was happening, and I told them exactly what Apple had discussed with me and what I'd seen and heard. Their response was, I need a divorce and a civil attorney. I'm sorry, but how is this civil? This is criminal. This is stalking. This is invasive. This has taken everything from me. It has changed me. I don't talk. I don't sit inside my home. I'm traumatized. I'm afraid to go into my bathroom. I'm forever changed in the age of technology, and I couldn't stand to be around it.

Rabbit Hole

I'd hoped to resolve this matter quickly. I felt I'd done all the things. I'd filed the police report, contacted the credit bureaus and notified them to freeze my credit. I contacted the FBI cyber crimes division, which is an online-only form, and I thought that was hilarious. How do they expect someone who's been hacked to receive their response via email? And much less be able to fill out the form without their device messing up?

I filed with the Federal Trade Commission. I followed their steps of what to do next. I notified the IRS. I notified every company down to the car insurance. I did everything I was supposed to in order to resolve this and I did it immediately.

Capital One was the only company that was able to help me or attempt to anyway. One day I received an email to one of the many email addresses I'd created during this time and it was from Walmart Grocery. When you get your groceries delivered, they always send a picture to your email showing you that they've left your order at your door.

This particular day I received a picture and knew it couldn't be my order because I had no way to order anything online, much less access my account with Walmart. The picture was of groceries in someone's back seat, not their doorstep. Clever.

I contacted Capital One because that's the credit card that was charged that day. They were able to tell me that is wasn't Walmart; it was, in fact, Amazon. It was for a gift card through Amazon. How they were able to tell that, I don't know. I just know that if Amazon looked like Walmart, then that means everything could look like something else.

How would I ever figure this out? I always knew the bank account would seem low, considering I worked a lot and didn't spend much, but when I'd look at the transactions, they seemed to be all the places we'd shop, so I never thought much of it other than, I can't believe we spent that much. When I worked shift work, it was like my brain never fully functioned. I was tired all the time and in zombie mode, as I called it.

I noticed things throughout the years with the bank account, but again, I'd looked and didn't see anything weird. That and who would ever think this would happen? I mean, come on, Walmart was Amazon! That's crazy to me! Capital One refunded over two thousand dollars that day to my card. In less than a week, it was maxed out. After the sixth time of this happening not only to this card but two others I had, I gave up.

I thought if they were all maxed out, then I won't have to deal with this anymore. My fight was starting to slow down. I was starting to realize just how bad it was. How long it'd been going on and how much money might've been taken over the years.

The thought of this occurring for so long overwhelmed me. I was at a loss for words. How was I going to continue fighting for my job, my money, my identity and my health all at the same time? Who can? I was losing hope and fast.

Each phone call would last hours at a time. You'd have to talk to the person that answered just for them to say, let me transfer you to the fraud department. I learned quickly to ask for the fraud department first. It saves some time, but not much.

One day I decided not only to pull my credit report but I wanted to run a background check on myself. Why not? Who knows what I would find that might help? I could've never imagined the rabbit hole I was about to go down.

I started with me. I didn't exist. On three different background check sites! I didn't exist. No record of me at all. Next was my husband. He was still claiming he'd been hacked, so why not? I discovered that his phone number was listed under his ex-wife and a different cellphone carrier. How is that possible? I also discovered that her email was listed as his. Who do you think I searched next? You guessed it, the ex.

I wasn't surprised anymore by what I found. She had over twenty names she went by. Her three ex-husbands and her current husband, her maiden name and even the last names of members of her extended family. Her background check had my husband's email listed and vice versa.

It was the most confusing mess I'd ever seen. I found myself doing this daily. I'd search all the phone numbers and email addresses that were listed for them. They both had many. They were so entangled with each other and yet, I, his wife, wasn't connected to him at all. Nor her husband to her.

What were they up to? How long has this been a thing? Did they always have this plan? Were they in it together as a felony family? It sure looked like it.

I reached out to an identity theft attorney one day at lunch. I asked them what they could do to help me. They explained they usually go after the companies that were supposed to protect you. For example, AT&T. We had a fraud prevention service added to our plan. I notified them in June something was off about the email I received. I'd called them twenty times.

So the attorney goes after the companies. I explained I knew who did this, and I had proof and they said we still go after the companies and then we could go after the individuals. I immediately asked for an appointment, but because I'd called during lunch they just took my name and number and I never heard back.

Not only did I not hear back, but I could no longer call them. My phone wouldn't let me. The second it would ring, my call was disconnected. This occurred with the IRS, mortgage company, Fidelity 401k, Wells Fargo and Amazon.

I literally couldn't speak to them. I couldn't go to their websites either. It wasn't long after that I asked my husband for a good old-fashioned land line. I wanted to make the phone calls and I needed them to be able to talk to me.

He agreed and went that day and bought cordless phones. He was so sweet about it. It came with four handsets. You know, so everyone could have one. He even set mine up outside, right next to me. Isn't that nice? Not so much.

It took one phone call asking if we were The Magic Ice Cream Shop for me to start looking at these phones. I realized they weren't land lines at all. He'd purchased cordless phones and had them connected to his xfinity account that he now had without me, and they ran off Wi-Fi. Wow. I felt so betrayed. He knew how afraid of Wi-Fi I was at this point.

I'd asked for a landline. One phone so I could have private conversations and instead, I got four phones that were basically cellphones.

One day not long after removing mine from outside and never using it again, I heard the oldest daughter talking in her room. That was weird because they were no longer allowed to have their phones at our home, per their mother. I walked into her room and asked who she was talking to. She said to her mom. I asked if she called her on the cordless phone and she answered no, she called here. Hmm, that's odd because I was standing in our kitchen surrounded by the other three phones, and they never rang.

I took the cordless phone from her at that point because, well, I didn't trust her, and I looked up the model number. I went through the call history and noticed something weird. It said baby monitor on several calls. Baby monitor? What?

The manual to the phone says you can use the handsets as baby monitors and even call the phones from another cell phone using this feature. It was our new Alexa as I called it. The mom could still drop into my home and everyone knew it but me.

I was so angry! I went to the garage, where my husband spent most of his time and I demanded to know why he would do this to me. He could see the toll it was taking. He didn't say anything; he just went and unplugged the phones and smashed them on the garage floor. That was his answer.

I cried so hard that night. Betrayal again. Four of them and one of me. How would I ever recover? The rabbit hole caused me to question myself and my sanity. I was thinking of the craziest things that happened to be true! I wasn't insane; my situation was. All the while, my husband tells me that everything I tell him that goes on doesn't make sense. He dismissed everything I'd say.

I quit talking after that.

Noted

Paying Attention

Ever have an experience when something happens, or someone makes a comment or acts differently and you think, hmm, that's weird?

You don't care enough to confront the situation right then, but you take note. File it away in your brain. I call mine the WTF files.

I reference them when needed. Example: if another situation similar pops up. Then I'll refer to the WTF files to help it make sense to me.

I have a habit of not ignoring things, but more like I give people the benefit of the doubt first before I address something.

Well, let's just say those files come in handy. Like when a neighbor talks to your husband and continues to message you randomly and unsolicited. Then you find out she's sent home meatballs for him and the kids, but not you. Noted.

Or when you notice an ex-wife of your husband constantly just showing up at your house unannounced and getting out of her car when she never used to. Noted.

When you can't speak to your husband about two particular women without him becoming irate. Noted.

As I'm writing this book, the files are flooding back in. I'm remembering so many things at once. They help fill in the gaps and make sense of things.

I didn't know that this was also a sign of trauma. I'd experienced past traumas prior to this situation, so what I was doing was "normal." I would compartmentalize the things I didn't want to face at the time, but I never forgot. I just tucked them away.

If something didn't feel right to me or something someone said didn't add up... noted.

I'm amazed at how good I was at this. I actually recently received a diagnosis of CPTSD. Where I've experienced multiple traumas. This explains my attitude towards things. Big things didn't affect me. I'm great in emergency situations, but small things were difficult for me.

So if you're someone that does this, maybe you should talk about why. Or just think about what happened in your life that caused you to take notes and not speak. I never looked at it that way until receiving therapy. I just thought I was exceptional.

D-Day

I Know Everything

July 24th, 2021. I call this day D Day. It was actually the day of the birthday party of my friend Lindsey's little girl. This day is very significant in my story. Here's why. I stayed up late again that night. I was used to working the night shift. I had done so for ten years at that point. So it was not unusual for me to stay up late. I stayed up late still trying to figure out what was going on in all of my accounts, still trying to gain access to emails, my Amazon account, and my AT&T account, and I think it was around 6:00 that morning, my phone started acting up really, really bad. I could hardly do anything about it.

At this point, I still thought that everyone in the house had been hacked and that it wasn't just me. So knowing this information, I immediately thought of my husband's work phone, his work cell phone that he kept at home on the weekends, and I didn't want anything to happen to that.

So I went over to his work cell phone to turn it off because I thought our Wi-Fi was messed up. And

I noticed that he had a ton of notifications on the home screen, and these weren't just any notifications. They didn't have anything to do with work at all. They were actually from his personal email address that he had signed in to on his work phone, which was weird. But the notifications that he was getting were the ones that I should have been getting for all of my accounts, like from the bank saying, hey, your password got changed, or, hey, your username has been changed.

So what I'd been staying up doing every night and looking for and trying to gain access to, he had the access. It was on his work phone, signed into his personal email address. Well, there's a passcode that you have to have to gain access to the work phone. I couldn't go through everything. I just freaked out silently because everyone in the house was still asleep. I didn't know why he would have this information or why he wouldn't have shared it with me. Why was I led to believe that this was happening to everyone, not just me? I didn't know what to do. I made myself a cup of coffee and went back outside, and shortly after, my youngest stepdaughter woke up, and she came outside with me, as she normally does, and that's our morning chats. We'd shared many morning chats. That was our time alone together. Our time to talk about whatever was on her mind. She'd been waking up in tears for weeks at this point. She would never tell me why other than she didn't know. She was just upset. I tried to comfort her as best as I could and just be there for her. I couldn't understand what was going on. Did she know too? Did she feel she had betrayed me?

We talked for about an hour, and I just couldn't contain myself anymore. I decided to go wake up my husband. I go into our bedroom, and I just nudge him, not lovingly in any way. I was angry and scared. I knew that he had been lying to me at that point. I knew that he had some involvement. I didn't know to what extent. I just knew what I saw. So I nudged him and said, "Hey, you need to get up." And he looked at me, confused and he said, "What's going on? Why? What's wrong?" And I just looked at him, and I said, "I know everything, and I want a divorce. Good morning." And I walked off and I went right back outside. He immediately started yelling, which is something I wasn't used to hearing from him. He never yelled. He never got mad, especially at me.

I go back outside with my youngest stepdaughter, and he comes busting through the door and says to my stepdaughter that she needs to go inside. Then he proceeded to close the blinds so that you couldn't see anything that was going on outside, which I noted.

I thought that was really odd. Why is he closing the blinds? That's weird. And he says to me, "What are you talking about you know everything?" And I just repeated myself. "I know everything." Because if there's one thing that I've learned in my life, it's that no one knows what's going on in your mind except for you, right? So if I tell him that I know everything, well to him, he really thinks that I must know everything. He freaked out. I mean, full-blown panic because he didn't know what that meant. And if I knew everything, well, that must be really, really bad the way he reacted.

So as I'm sitting there on the outside sofa drinking my coffee, he's yelling and screaming at me that I've lost my mind. That he was concerned this would happen and that he needed to call my psychiatrist. He needed to call both of my friends that are nurses. He needed to call an ambulance. He's then opening the door to the inside of the house, yelling at the kids to get in the car, hurry, pack a bag, get in the car, they needed to leave.

He gets down on his hands and knees in front of me, and he places his hands on my knees. He looks me in the eye, and he says to me, "You're scaring me. I don't understand. You're scaring me. I think you've lost it. You cannot go to this party with us. You need to take your ass inside and go to bed, and you better be your ass in the bed when I get back from that party. I need to call an ambulance. You need help. You've lost your mind."

Right there at that moment, I knew that he wasn't kidding. This was plan B; this was his plan if I ever did find out what was going on. That's how I felt and I knew that's what it was. I didn't say another word, at least not right then. But the dramatics of it all blew my mind. And he just kept repeating, "You haven't slept. You haven't slept. You don't know what you're talking about."

This is funny because all the years that I worked shift work and all the years that I worked the night shift and I couldn't sleep and I would come home in the morning and I'd get home at 6:30 AM and I'd still be awake at 10:30 AM. There were many, many nights over, many, many years that I didn't sleep. He never showed concern. So why, all of a sudden, did this night mean that I needed an ambulance? Was it because of what I'd said?

"I know everything." And he didn't know what that meant or where I got my information from. I didn't tell him. I didn't tell him anything about his cell phone. I didn't tell him anything about what I saw, and I didn't dig into it because it scared me, to be honest. I saw all I needed to see at that moment for me to know that I was the only one hacked and that he potentially had something to do with it. Or at least he knew what was going on because he was receiving the email notifications that I should have been receiving and he was keeping that information from me.

The day before this happened, and I don't know why I said this, but Lindsey called wanting to know would we make it to the birthday party. Of course, we would've made it to the birthday party! We always went to every function as a family when I was available and not working. For whatever reason, I made the comment I will be there. I don't know about them, speaking of my husband and my stepdaughters, but I will be there. I made sure to stress that to her, and I didn't know why I needed to do that at the time.

I was so thankful that I did because, you see, there was no way he was going to that party with his kids without me and no one notice or expect me. He loaded his kids up, took them to the birthday party, and I stayed home.

When he left, I immediately started rummaging through the house. I've never done that before. Everybody's stuff is their stuff. I'm not nosy in that way. I never have been. But I started finding all kinds of flash drives and I found a recording device that was magnetic and was under our grill outside where I sat. I took everything that I could because I didn't understand what these things were. I took them all and I hid them. I hid them in coat pockets. I never put anything in the same place together. Everything was spread out. So spread out that, to this day, I still don't know where everything is.

I called Summer; we'd been friends for 25 years at this point. After finding the recording device on the grill, I didn't know where I could be heard or where I could be seen. I'd already had the Alexa moment. So now I'm dealing with finding a recording device on my grill. I'm dealing with seeing that my husband has information that he's withholding from me and trying to act like he needs to have me locked up for mental reasons. I call Summer and I'm calling her from inside my closet and I'm whispering to her, and she told me to go to bed. She said it sounded like I needed some sleep and I needed to go to bed. She agreed with my husband, and we got off the phone.

And right there at that moment, I didn't know what I was going to do. Who was going to believe me if not my friend of 25 years? Who was going to help me when he came home from the birthday party if he had me put away in a mental hospital? Who would hear me? I was frantic. I was scared. I didn't know whether I needed to leave. I had not been asleep at that point. That's true. I shouldn't have been driving. I didn't know where to go. I didn't know what to do or who to trust. I was shaking, physically shaking, and I thought to myself, I have another friend. I have another friend at the party. Let me call her. I'm going to give it one more shot. I go outside, way off into the backyard, into the corner of the yard. Again, I'm worried that I will be recorded or he'll see me. I don't know where any cameras or recording devices are at this point, and it wouldn't be surprising if they were all over the place. I didn't know. I was completely paranoid.

I called Leslie and I explained to her what I had seen and what was going on, and she said, "Brooke, you're hysterical." And I was, absolutely. I just cried just this gut-wrenching, deep down from your soul cry because I felt like no one could hear me. No one's listening to me. They all think that I'm crazy, and I'm not crazy. This happened to me. This is real and I have proof of it. But then she said something else right after that. So what felt like 10 minutes of silence was actually only half of a second. And she said, "But rightfully so, Brooke. Rightfully so, you're hysterical." And I cannot tell you the relief that came over my body at that moment. My whole entire body completely relaxed, and I slumped down on the swing outside because someone had heard me, someone was listening to me, and they believed me.

Yes, I was hysterical and I was afraid that he was going to come back and have me locked up in a mental hospital. Leslie got off the phone with me because she wanted to go see what was going on with him at the party. She had gone to a bathroom to have this private conversation with me. Nobody knew that she had been on the phone with me at all. And when she walks outside, she notices that Summer, the one that told me to go to bed, had just pulled up at the party and immediately goes straight to my husband and they're having a deep conversation.

So everybody is kind of looking around at each other, like, what's going on? Where is Brooke? And my husband was asked where I was. Well, he told Lindsey, who I'd spoken to the day before, who I told that I would be there and everyone else that I had worked the night before and I was asleep. She knew that wasn't right because she had talked to me the day before. I'd made it clear to her. So he goes on mingling through the party, and he has another deep conversation with another woman. We'll call her Kay. But this woman is not a friend of mine. This woman was a neighbor of mine. She was an acquaintance of mine. She was a friend of a friend. She was not one to me, and here my husband was in deep conversation.

The interesting thing about my husband talking to Kay was that he would always ask what her name was. At every event. He would bother me with, "what's that girl's name again"? So they shouldn't know each other enough to be having an intense conversation, as Lindsey described it.

Lindsey, who's hosting the party, decides to walk up and ask them what they're talking about. It was obvious to her that this was not normal. And also, where's Brooke? So immediately when she walked up, they quit talking. And she mentioned that to them. Why did you all quit talking? You seemed to be in deep conversation. And they didn't say another word.

While all of this is taking place, I'm at home throwing clothes in a bag and deciding where to go and how much time I have to leave. I was texting everyone I thought might be there, asking them to let me know when he left. I wanted to be gone before he arrived. I don't recall anyone answering me, so I was home when him and my step daughters arrived home.

He'd seen I hadn't been to sleep. The kids got in the pool. It was a hot day, after all. My husband and I are in the kitchen. He started yelling at me again. He wanted to let me know that he could have me locked up and with my family history of mental health issues, cheap shot, I know, that they would keep me. It was as if he wanted to let me know that in my hysteria and combined with the history of seeing a psychiatrist that it wouldn't be a problem.

He told me to get the fuck out of "his" house. His house? When did that happen? I was the borrower on the mortgage, him the co-borrower, but ok. I was scared and he said I was scaring his children and I couldn't be around them. I grabbed my bag and left. I didn't know where to go or who to trust. I was running on adrenaline at this point. I couldn't think clearly. I was a mess.

I pulled into a local grocery store parking lot and let the tears fall. The kind of tears that come with gut-wrenching sounds. The kind that sounds like you've lost someone dear. The kind that sounds like you can't go on. My phone starts ringing off the hook. It was Summer, Summer's mom and Leslie. I answered for Leslie. She'd listened to me. I felt safe with her.

She told me the party had wrapped up and to come to Lindsey's and we could talk in private. So that's what I did. When I arrived, I walked in through the front; everyone goes to the back to be sure no one sees me. We walked into Lindsey's room, where I collapsed on the floor. I was drained. I was exhausted from the emotion. I sat on the floor, legs crossed, for about fifteen minutes with Leslie by my side.

She calmed me down enough to tell her what was going on. Shortly after, Lindsey walked in and she encouraged me to come outside in the garage and talk. When we walked into the garage, Kay was sitting there alone in a chair. Why? Why was she still there? Alone in the garage? Weird. Noted.

As Leslie, Lindsey and I begin talking, Kay gets up and leaves without speaking to me. This was odd. We'd all stopped and noticed this, but she wasn't important to me and at this point, I didn't know about the deep conversation with my husband, so I ignored it but noted it.

Lindsey then tells me about the conversation she walked up on. I still ignored it. That was the least of my problems, right? No. Kay was a factor; I just didn't know it yet.

Lindsey offered for me to spend the night at her home. She fed me and made the sofa up for me. Before going to bed, I sat in the garage talking with Leslie, Lindsey and her husband. Lindsey's husband and my husband had grown close over the past three years. We'd vacationed together twice in 2019.

He was confused as to what was going on but made some comments that night that were unfamiliar to me about my husband. He said he was into stocks. Stocks? No, he wasn't. Not to my knowledge. That was weird and I didn't pay much attention to it other than, you guessed it, noted.

The next morning I woke up refreshed. I'd had a good night's sleep in a place I felt safe and was able to eat. Lindsey made me breakfast casserole which is one of my favorites. I needed to go home and shower, so that's just what I did. I went home. I walked straight to the bathroom and closed the door. We had a walk-in shower with a door. While showering, my husband came in yelling at me about where I'd been. He told me to get out of "his" house, so why the interest in where I'd been?

He opened the door to the shower and continued questioning me. As I stood there cold from the door being opened, he interrogated me. When was the last time you spoke to your psychiatrist? Does she know what shape you're in? I assured him I'd kept appointments and actually increased those visits from every six months to once weekly, and if he thought for one second I hadn't discussed him or what was going on, then he was mistaken. I wanted him to know that he couldn't call her. I'd already removed him as my emergency contact and my doctor was aware of what the police said.

I wanted him to know putting me in a mental hospital wasn't as easy as he'd thought. He wanted to know what I knew. I refused to talk and asked him to leave me alone. He wouldn't. He NEEDED to know what I knew. I was afraid, but after a good night's rest, I could think more clearly and carefully about what I'd say next.

I wanted him to know I was not weak. I'm not broken. I'm a fighter and a survivor, and I won't stop until I get to the bottom of this. So while standing there naked and cold and arguing in the bathroom, I told him that he messed up by thinking he could go to my friend's home and think anyone would believe the excuses he gave as to why I wasn't there. He asked me to elaborate. As I said, this was an interrogation.

I explained that he went to the party and was engaged in deep conversations with Summer and Kay. Kay! Kay! He yelled at me. What was I talking to her about? I said, well, idk because I wasn't there. He completely flipped out. Once I said her name, it was over. He stormed out of the bathroom, slamming the door so hard I thought it'd fall. I closed the shower door and finished up.

It was maybe a week later that I received a Facebook message from Kay. She wanted to let me know that she had no ill intentions with my husband and that their conversation was about the tough season "he" was going through and how "the poor guy was almost in tears."

Okay, why is she messaging me? Why is she letting me know that my husband confides in her? He doesn't even remember her name. So I ignored that message and gave no response because, in my mind, I didn't have time for nonsense. It didn't deserve a response. Why would it? She sounded desperate, and I had to work the next day.

The next week after that, I received another message on Facebook, but this time Kay included my husband. She wants to know if she could bring her daughter to our home to swim.

I ignored this message as well. I thought I'd made myself clear about where she ranked in my life and how unimportant she was. So I left the chat. FB notifies all parties in the chat when someone leaves. "Brooke left the chat." That was my answer.

While I was swimming in the pool, my husband came outside after just waking up. It was mid-day. It's hot. He immediately starts yelling at me as to why I ignored Kay. I responded very simply; she's obviously crazy because she won't stop messaging me about you and your feelings and how you confide in her. Well, that wasn't the right answer because the fight that occurred after that with him screaming at me in the backyard, where I knew all the neighbors could hear, was so bad that I packed a bag and went to my sister Audra's house.

Not even an hour later, Kay and her daughter arrived at my home. I messaged Kay letting her know I was not there and would not be there. What woman lets her teenage daughter stay unsupervised by a man she doesn't know? Kay does.

Kay's daughter spent the night in my home that night without me there. I was told she'd be gone come morning. Well, at 3:00 in the afternoon the next day, I asked my husband if I could come home. I wanted a shower and to brush my teeth.

When I arrived home around 5:00 pm, Kay's daughter was still there. I asked my youngest step daughter why she was still there and she told me that they'd all had breakfast at Kay's house that morning, and Kay was gone shopping.

We lived at the entrance to our neighborhood. This meant that everyone coming and going would need to pass our home. I sat outside on the front steps waiting for her car to pass. I sat there for 5 hours, and she never drove by.

At 10:00 pm, my stepdaughters and Kays's daughter come outside and start walking to Kay's house. I asked them what they were doing. It was pitch black outside and three little girls shouldn't be walking alone. They explained Kay was now home, and they were going to eat dinner because she'd cooked for them. I offered to escort them and my husband interjected they'll be fine. The overprotective dad is now very comfortable with letting this occur.

I waited on my back porch for them to come back home and we had a giant window that would let me see straight through the house to the front door. I was on a three-way call with Leslie and Lindsey when they walked in the door about an hour later. I put my phone down and ran to the front of the house like a track star. I wanted to know if Kay was out there. She was. In her mini blue Jean skirt.

I asked her why she wasn't going to come to the door and speak to me. She explained she didn't know I was home as she stood next to my car. I was enraged. I told her that this car she was standing next to was mine and she knew that! I told her to get the hell off my property immediately and to not ever return! She looked at me with her lips pressed together and shook her head in kind of a round nodding motion as if she was just letting me say what I needed to, but she knew she'd be back. She reached in to hug me. Hug me?! What? What's wrong with this bitch I thought. Get the hell away from me is how I responded.

She eventually left walking on foot as she lived just a few houses down. When I went back inside, my husband looked at me as if I'd lost my mind again. The nerve of them both.

While cleaning the kitchen that night, I'd discovered she'd sent my husband home with spaghetti and meatballs. Meatballs! I hate meatballs and where the Hell was mine? What was going on here? I, that night, for the first time ever, cussed in front of the children. I let everyone know I better not ever see another MF'n meatball in my home!

The next day my husband and the youngest child went to a local home store. The oldest was left with me without asking. She was more than happy to tell me all about the fun day spent with Kay the day before. I only asked her one question since her memory seemed to be excellent in recalling that day. I asked if Kay had been inside our home. She immediately suffered memory loss and couldn't recall anything else and quickly got up and walked back inside.

Noted.

Meatball Goofin' Dude

The Chameleon Effect

The chameleon effect is an unknowing mimic of other people's behaviors. You know how when you're around someone long enough, you start to pick up their sayings and mannerisms? You can't help it. Or like when a really annoying commercial comes on over and over and you find yourself singing that tune later? Yeah. I hate that. It's the worst.

I don't like meatballs. Not in spaghetti, anyway. Who wants a chunk of meat like that? I hate meatballs. I actually choked on one once. Could Kay have known this? Is this why I didn't get an invite or a to-go plate? I doubt that.

Dude. Ugh. Dude. Why? Well, the lady neighbor says dude, dude. One day my husband called me dude. Dude?!!! Thats what I thought! I know he doesn't say this. I would've tried to correct that years ago, dude!

Goofin'. Now I know that people say this. But I only knew of one at the time before my husband started using it. Sweet young thing at work. Isn't that nice?

I've always been able to pick up on things that are out of the ordinary and these were no exception. The second I heard the words leave his mouth, I knew he'd been talking to someone that I wasn't that familiar with.

Point is, I hate meatballs. You're not fooling anyone, Dude. Stop Goofin'.

Bathroom Camera Two

That's right. Bathroom Camera 2. It wasn't long after I discovered Wi-Fi on my car that one day, while in my driveway, I saw my car trying to connect to bathroom camera 2.

I was immediately freaked out. For several reasons. One, I'd already had the Alexa incident while I was in the bathroom. Two, who the hell has a camera in their bathroom? Three, where the hell is bathroom camera 2?! I mean, we had three bathrooms. Which one was 2? Or was it the second camera in one bathroom?!

I never said anything to my husband about this because I quit telling him anything weird going on because his response was always, "That doesn't make any sense." And then, of course, the emails he hid from me.

So I took a picture of my car and sent it to at least four people that day. It was something I'd gotten in the habit of doing since this all started. If I saw something weird, I'd take a picture or a screenshot and send them to people so if my photos disappeared again, someone would have the evidence.

What I couldn't have planned for was the mental toll this would take on me. Between the Alexa and Bathroom Camera 2, which I never found, I could barely go into the bathrooms.

My friends didn't even want to go to my bathrooms. Eventually, I would have to shower. I was so used to showering in the mornings and washing my hair and at night, I'd take a bubble bath to relax before bed. I'd had the same routine for the majority of my life.

This situation interrupted that routine tremendously. I would go days without showering and longer before I could wash my hair. If I washed my hair, it meant a longer shower. To me, that was torture. I didn't want to be in the bathroom naked. Ever again. Not any bathroom anywhere.

After this incident, my weight dropped even more. I was down to 102 lbs. I looked unrecognizable. I could barely look at myself in the mirror. I knew something had to change. My friends were even used to me not bathing at that point.

My stepmom gave me the number to a trauma therapist and I called immediately. I had a broken foot at the time because, let's be honest, there weren't many times my foot wasn't broken at this point. It was my right foot this time and I couldn't drive, so my husband drove me to my trauma appt.

I knew no matter how uncomfortable it would be to say what I had to say with him nearby, I had to say it. The therapist helped me bathe again. Now it's still not like the routine I'd had my whole life, but I could get through the process easier.

I was able to use the restroom at other people's homes without freaking out and wondering if they had cameras too.

I'm not ashamed to tell anyone what this did to me or how it affected me and in what ways. The brain is an amazing thing. I, for the better part of two years, was in shock. I'd figured out how to "deal" with what happened and was continuing to happen to me without having a breakdown.

I'll always believe it's because I talked about it. I told anyone that would listen to me. I knew everyone thought I was insane because how could I make them understand things I didn't even understand? All I could do was tell them what I knew.

To sit in silence outside of my home because I couldn't stand to be inside a place I felt my privacy was so violated after Alexa and then not being able to at least shower was horrible.

I was able to understand what trauma was, how it affects our bodies and how I can cope in a healthier manner. Did it "fix me"? No. Did it help me rationalize situations better? Absolutely. But trauma, for me so far, will always be there. My therapist suggested EMDR.

Eye Movement Desensitization and Reprocessing (EMDR) is a psychotherapy treatment that was originally designed to alleviate the distress associated with traumatic memories. I referred to it as "tapping it out."

My therapist believed that I would be able to do a series of tapping methods throughout my day and the trauma would eventually go away. It's a grounding technique. A reminder that you're safe. But how did I know I was safe? I would get anxious just thinking I had to even do it.

I didn't stick with it and my therapist didn't stick with me. It was tap it out or nothing. Is this the only solution? I sure hope not. As a therapist, I would think I'd stay the course with my patient. Not give up on them. My therapist said if I wouldn't do the EMDR, then she didn't think she could help me and I needed to go back to my psychiatrist. I'd been seeing one since 2009 after a bad car wreck. I developed severe anxiety after that trauma.

I was happy to see my psychiatrist. She knew me. She believed me. She understood me. I spoke to her weekly for months. She truly is an angel on Earth. She's helped me in more ways than she'll ever know and I'm forever grateful to her.

My mother was also very helpful during this time. She would meditate on the phone with me, pray for me when I cried so hard I couldn't pray for myself and was there to listen to me. One day she asked me where I thought the camera was in the bathroom. I told her the air vent and I couldn't reach it even with a ladder. She told me to cover it up or close it and take my shower in peace. I did. Thank you Mom.

The point is, I came to the conclusion that if there was a camera, it's already seen all it possibly could, so who cares and when you're dealing with trauma, it truly is mind over matter.

Hammer Time

I Needed A Break

One afternoon in late July of 2021, I'd been sitting on the back porch, which was my new normal and my husband came and sat beside me with his laptop. My cellphone started messing up so badly that I couldn't use it at all. By this time, I was semi-used to it. I wouldn't cry or cuss anymore. But this particular day, I'd had enough. And anyone who knows me knows that it really takes a lot to get me upset. I'd had enough this day. I calmly stood up and said in a low voice, that's it, and walked to the garage, cell phone in hand.

I knew exactly what I was going to do. I walked over to the toolbox, found a hammer and set my phone on the ground and whack! Whack! Whack! I'd taken care of the problem. No more trouble with my phone because there no longer was one. I grabbed the shop vac and started vacuuming the glass and I noticed my husband standing at the top of the steps in the garage with a very disturbed look on his face. How long had he been standing there? Did he watch the whole thing? I don't know, but I turned to him after cleaning my mess and told him I'd be going for a drive and if anything in my car looks like it's connected to Wi-Fi, I was bringing the hammer to solve that problem too.

Well, that's just what I did. I made it two miles down the road and sure enough, my car was connected to something. I couldn't look at anymore. I'd called the dealership for help and my brother-in-law and I went through every part of the car we could think of, looking for any devices. The dealership said they couldn't disconnect it without the device it was connected to. I didn't have it because I didn't do it. So I pulled over on the side of the road and I got my hammer and whack! Whack! To the display screen that lets me operate the radio and navigation.

I know you probably think that's a little much. Maybe I went overboard that day, but that's the thing, I don't feel like I did. The relief I felt after doing that was greatly needed. I was at peace. I know it didn't solve the problem, but I didn't have to look at it. I went and met Leslie at Lindsey's house right after. I calmly told her what I did. She listened, maybe even laughed. Leslie and I sat by the pool the rest of that afternoon, catching up and enjoying being able to talk privately with each other.

When I arrived home, my husband was outside in the garage and the garage door was open, so he saw me pull up. He looked inside the car and said I can't believe you did that! I just kept walking into the house straight to my back porch. He followed me, yelling about how crazy that was and how expensive it'll be to fix it. I assured him I would not be fixing it and not to worry. I kept that hammer with me for a while after that. Just in case.

Doubtful Detectives

Identity Theft Times Two

On August 4, 2021, my husband and I were called in by the detectives at the police station to bring in our devices and provide proof for my identity case. This was one of the hardest days I'd been through. It was a hot Summer day and I'd broken my left foot the day before and had to go to the orthopedic doctor that morning. I was in a tremendous amount of pain.

It was that day I discovered something wrong with my health insurance. My fractures only required an orthopedic boot to wear and as they sent me to the room to get fitted for it, the nurse walked in and told me that my deductible hadn't been met. So this means a forty-dollar boot would actually cost me five hundred. What?! Are you kidding me? How is it August and my deductible hasn't been met? I've seen several doctors that year. There was no reason why it shouldn't have been met. Red flag!

I was so upset and in pain that I ended up just telling my husband to take me to the car. We left, broken toe and metatarsal and no boot to secure it. Thankfully I already owned a pair of crutches because I couldn't put the weight down without the boot and because of the GI issues I was having, they couldn't prescribe pain meds.

I was in tears. Tears from the pain and tears from the frustration with the insurance. We left the doctor and went straight to the police department. I was in so much pain at this point because I hadn't been able to prop my foot up for several hours and I was shaking. I was beginning to feel defeated.

The detectives decided to split us up that day, my husband and I. They called me back first. I wasn't sure how to feel about that. It's odd, right? That's what I thought as they walked me down the hall to their office. When I got back there, they had a video camera set up and I noticed it immediately. I'd already spoken to them once before, so I knew that wasn't there before. I immediately asked, what's that for? One of the detectives, there were two, both female, explained it was for the district attorney. I thought that's awesome! They're going to do something about this! I felt relief!

The very first question they asked me was, why did I have the children on my Aflac policy? Huh? What in the world did that have to do with anything at all?! But, I'd never been interrogated before, other than my husband, and that's what was happening. I'd watched the ID channel enough to know that at any point, you can get up and leave without answering questions, but I didn't understand, I was in pain, and also, I had nothing to hide. So I answered their questions. For forty-five minutes, I answered the most absurd questions that I never thought I would be asked and had nothing to do with me or my identity theft.

I told them I had an Aflac policy when I was single and when I got married, I added my husband and Aflac explained I could add my step children as well. So I did. Why not? It helped cover medical costs that we had to pay anyway. The detectives are writing and filming as I talk. What were they even writing? None of this made sense and I was growing very defensive and uncomfortable at this point and my foot was swollen and throbbing at this point.

The next question was, and get ready for this one because I was not, but why was I trying to adopt the children? What?! Why was I trying to adopt the children?!! I wish I could see the footage from that day because I'm sure my facial expression was shock. What are they talking about? I thought. I said, why in the world would I be trying to adopt the kids when they have two parents and two step-parents? That's absurd. I didn't have any of my own; I can have children, it was a personal choice not to. I then said I'm sorry. What does this have to do with my identity theft?

One of the detectives then opened a file that was at least an inch thick and I could see a giant printout of the ex-wife's driver's license. So they had a huge file on her? I don't know. Was it just for show? Who knows! It was all so confusing. I understand now how people get intimidated in these situations. They catch you off guard.

I was then asked what I'd been told about a 911 call to the ex-wife's house regarding a domestic dispute. Well, I hadn't been told anything. I'd actually heard the recording of a conversation between my husband and the ex-wife's husband. The ex's husband called my husband to explain his concern for the children due to the abusive behavior of the ex-wife. I told this to the detectives. Her husband told her what had happened. The detectives both look at me and shake their heads no. No? What do you mean no? No, it didn't happen? No I didn't hear that? No, that's incorrect? I asked all of these questions and they did not respond but continued with the interrogation and note-taking.

The next thing was not actually a question, but them letting me know I was a problem. A problem? How? I work and come home and do everything for everyone. I've never said anything to the ex-wife or the children that was wrong. We'd never argued. So, I'm sorry but how am I a problem? I asked. They told me there was footage of me. What footage? And if so, well that just proves my point that I'm being recorded without my knowledge!

They explained that my husband and his ex-wife were having secret conversations about custody. They explained that I was the main issue. Me. I laughed. It was so ridiculous to me. The ex-wife ran our home. She made the decisions in my house, so how was I a problem?! If anyone was a problem, it was her! They told me I interfered with the relationship between the mother and the kids, the kids and the dad and the mom and dad discussing their kids. If anything, the ex interfered in my relationships with them.

Hmmmm, that's the craziest thing anyone could say to me because I'd been putting up with all of their bullshit for almost ten years at this point, so when did this "problem" start? And why are the conversations a secret? This made zero sense to me. If I crossed a boundary, it was an invisible boundary made up of ten years in.

After 45 minutes of questions I never thought I'd be asked in my life and accusations that were incredibly false, they turned the camera off.

This is the part when my life changed. My real identity. My identity as a person. One detective looks at me and says your husband is a narcissist, he's a liar, a cheater and you need to be afraid of him. Afraid?! What? Why? I asked. She said that I was Julia Roberts in the movie Sleeping with The Enemy. She said they have a cop car out back and would take me home while they talked to my husband so I could grab a few belongings and they'd escort me to the Penelope House.

The Penelope House is a shelter for battered women and children. I told them I wouldn't go. I'm not afraid of my husband. I'd never even seen him angry. We didn't argue. Not really. I didn't recall D Day at the moment. I'm not sure why. They told me what they had to say to him was going to piss him off and make him angry and asked me if I was sure I didn't want to go. I was sure. What were they even talking about?

One detective said we don't want to end up hearing about you on the news or a crime podcast. This man is dangerous and unpredictable. They explained when a man is physically abusive, you know what to expect from him. But when a man is a narcissist, they're unpredictable, like Scott Peterson, who killed his pregnant wife, Lacy Peterson. This still didn't register for me. Why? Well, I know why. They just spent forty-five minutes questioning my character, and none of what they said was true. So why would I believe anything else they said? I know why. It's because what they were saying about me I knew wasn't true. It was me they were saying it to.

As I'm gathering my crutches and purse, they said, oh and by the way, we don't believe the explanation you gave on how you broke your foot. They thought my husband had done that to me. He hadn't. I couldn't wait to leave. This had nothing to do with my identity theft. It was a waste of my time. I was angry, I was in pain and I was confused. I was hurt. I couldn't believe I was being accused of trying to adopt the children. It felt like identity theft times two.

As I went back to the lobby, they called my husband back. I sat in the lobby, trying to process what had just taken place. I had so many emotions and I was on the verge of tears. I wanted to go home. In less than five minutes, he came storming out, slammed open the door and was yelling and cussing the detectives. He said I want my shit back! And proceeds to walk out the door to his truck, leaving me with crutches in the lobby. The detectives and I look at each other. Them with an I told you so look and me with shock.

My husband walks back in, now remembering that he'd left me in the lobby. He helped me up and carried my purse to the truck. While on the ride to a friend's house to get my car, driven home the day before by Leslie's daughter from urgent care because I couldn't drive with my broken foot, my husband asked me what the police said to me. Well, they told me not to tell him and to also quit digging for information, especially related to my place of employment.

I tried to act as calm as possible because now I was afraid. Now I've seen him angry. Now I'm recalling D Day. Now what they said was true in a sense. So I was scared and didn't know what to expect. I answered with nothing; I just had to sign forms and turn over my laptop, cellphone, AirPods, Apple Watch and flash drives. I asked him what they said to him because he was so angry and he said they're not going to fucking help us and that's all I was told. I rode in silence the rest of the way, wondering how am I the problem and why am I scared. What were they talking about? Where did they come up with these absurd questions and why is no one addressing what she did to me?

As we arrive at Leslie's, her daughter brings out an orthopedic boot and a scooter I could use. Usually, my husband would've just left after he saw I was in the car, but instead, he waited. He watched.

I wrote on a piece of paper what the police said and tried to hand it to the daughter, but my husband was watching the whole time. I had a pistol in my glove box that I told Leslie's husband to take and lock up for me because I didn't trust it being in the home. It was my intuition. I told her daughter that I'm going to throw the note from my window when I pulled off and grab it. I needed someone to know what I was told.

As I proceeded to leave, my husband followed me all the way home. Watching my every move. As soon as I got home, I put on my swimsuit and got in the pool. I didn't know what to think or do. I didn't know my place as a wife or stepmom anymore. That day stole my identity in a different way. It took away who I was as a person.

My husband had an errand to run and when he left, I called my dad. I told him the outrageous questions I'd been asked by the detectives and then I told him I was Julia Roberts. He asked me if I was afraid and I said, well, I don't know. I did know. I was. Of what? I don't know. He asked what I wanted to do. Well, the detectives told me the only way they'd help me is if I got a civil attorney and even suggested, hang on to your seats for this one, that I call the ex-wife and talk to her to help shed some light on the situation! So my dad said okay, let's get the attorney. So that was the plan.

The next day I had to go back to work despite their policy of you not being able to work if you're in a cast or boot of any kind. They broke their own policies all the time. That day was really hard for me. I was in a new position at my company. I'd been there over ten years at this point, but only two months in the department I was now working in. I arrived at work to discover my coworkers had boxes blocking my desk. I worked in Central Receiving, so we'd get all the packages to the site in our office. These weren't lightweight, either. So with my broken foot, I moved box after box just to be able to access my desk. No one helped. I was in pain without medication. I was at work doing things I shouldn't be. Lifting heavy boxes on an unstable foot with no help against their own policy.

Another coworker that was in my building, not my department, stopped me as I walked past her to the drink machine. She said she'd watched me deteriorate over the last few months and she was concerned. She advised me to file FMLA and go home and heal and deal with the private issues of identity theft. I filed immediately. I needed to do just that. So I did, except the issues weren't really private matters. See, they involved the company I worked for as well.

It wasn't long after that I discovered a picture on my phone that was not mine. One of the things that happen when another device is signed into your Apple ID is that the pictures can duplicate and transfer to the other device. So I found odd pictures on my phone that I knew I didn't take. One day not long after being home on FMLA, I noticed a very, very important picture in my album.

It was a picture of a computer screen in a crane in the warehouse at the company I worked for. Well, I didn't work in the warehouse, nor did I operate a crane. As I examined the picture further, I noticed it was a picture of my personal Gmail account and in the middle of the screen were the Wi-Fi connection options. So this told me exactly what warehouse, date and time this occurred. I couldn't believe it! I felt like I'd won the lottery!

I immediately called my IT dept at work and told them about the picture. They said no problem, we can identify the user. I texted the picture to three different IT guys and then I got a phone call. It was IT security. I didn't even know we had such a thing! He agreed that it wouldn't be a problem to identify the person and they'd let me know. I never heard from them again.

They knew what was wrong with my laptop. They knew my husband had something to do with the e-mail issue on the laptop and now they quit talking to me. Who was this person? Was someone other than my husband and his ex involved? Obviously. And they worked with me. And my job did nothing to protect me.

One of my favorite parts about this is that the CEO of the company made a YouTube video in November of 2021 discussing the company's zero tolerance for cyber fraud. The entire IT dept, HR department and multiple coworkers were aware of my situation. No one helped me. They knew about the police report. They chose to protect someone instead of helping me. What were they hiding? Insurance fraud? Tax fraud? Yes, and who knows what else. I worked for one of the largest steel mills in the world. I tried to find an attorney, but they owned every attorney I'd called, even out of state. I felt helpless, to say the least.

About four days after being interrogated for what I now referred to as the ex-wife's fake custody disagreement instead of my identity theft investigation, I decided to call her as advised by the detectives. I drove to a gas station nearby and used a burner phone and stood outside of my vehicle to make sure no one would know and even asked her not to mention the conversation because the detectives said I was in danger.

She, of course, offered no help. Her husband didn't even know she had talked to the police. She didn't shed light on anything but her ability to lie. I was so angry at the detectives to even suggest I call this horrible person that should've been arrested already to get answers!? Why would she tell me anything? It made no sense.

When I arrived home after calling the ex-wife, the five-minute drive, my husband knew of the call. She'd texted him and said, someone needs help, referring to me! What? How did I need help? Well, my husband was so angry at me. He called me a "cunt bitch". I'd never been called that in my life! Why was he so angry? Why did she tell when I clearly expressed my fear to her? If anything had happened to me that day, it would've been her fault and clearly, she was okay with that.

Obviously, my husband and his ex were having conversations and they seemed very loyal to each other. I, at one point during that interrogation, said, If there are private conversations being had, it makes more sense to me that the ex was listening into our home, well because she was, and she caught my husband doing something he shouldn't have been and was blackmailing him. That made perfect sense to me. It's the kind of person she was. It was always about money. And she never let go of my husband.

I was left trying to figure out everything myself. The who, what, where, when, why and how. Me. Just me. No one would help. Not the cellphone company, not the insurance company, not my HR or IT dept at my job that both my husband and I worked for. No attorneys. No one.

My health declined further after this. How could it not?

The Frog

Gaslit

It was hard for me to hear that I've been through a traumatic event. Not just this one, but multiple. It's called CPTSD.

The first time I told my psychiatrist what was going on with me, my sister by my side, I told her exactly every detail. I thought I did good! I didn't leave anything out.

Her response was, Brooke, the words coming out of your mouth do not match the emotions. I was like, huh? I just told you what happened to me. She explained it like a frog in a pot of boiling water. I'd never heard this phrase and asked her to elaborate as I was feeling defensive.

She explained that if you put a frog in a pot of boiling water, it will immediately jump out. It knows that water is dangerous. However, if you put a frog in room temperature water and slowly crank up the heat, the frog is still comfortable. That's what happened to me.

My therapist explained it as learned helplessness. I'd become this person that apologizes all the time. I tip-toed around. I tried to make myself small and unnoticeable. Why?

My sister had to educate me on this. I mean, sure, I was familiar with the word narcissist, but I didn't understand it. I didn't know that I was a victim of narcissistic abuse. I was, for lack of a better term, brainwashed.

It was a slow process. It took years. Years of someone never believing anything I said. Years of someone telling me I'm wrong or that didn't happen. Years of being told I have dementia because I don't remember things.

I remember one day asking my psychiatrist if I had dementia. I really believed I could. My husband and I often watched shows and movies together. We'd wait for the other one to be off work just so we could watch together.

Every time we would pick a movie, if I suggested one, he'd say, "We've already seen that, Brooke." But I knew I hadn't. But he'd convince me that we had. Go into telling me all about the movie until I'd say, "Oh yeah, I remember now."

One particular day and I think this was the moment I realized something wasn't right with the way he spoke to me, but every time I would shower, the water would get cold. I mentioned this to my husband because we had a tankless water heater and it should never be cold.

I knew that the temperature could be adjusted in the hallway on the control panel. I asked him to have someone come out and fix it. He said, "The water never gets cold for me," looked at his children and said, "Does it get cold for you guys?"

They both said no.

I knew at that moment that this was what he had done to me. I was telling him my water was cold and he chose to tell me it wasn't. This was what I was used to, but this day something clicked and I thought, who gives a shit about if your water isn't?! Mine is. Get it fixed and also, if I tell you something, then listen to me! I didn't say that, of course, because I'd become used to not speaking up.

I found myself not saying anything at all anymore about it. Why even talk, I thought. So I stopped. I stopped talking about anything and everything. I wouldn't check the mail. I wouldn't watch tv, and I wouldn't eat dinner. I didn't shop for groceries or necessities. I simply just stopped.

I'd sit on the back porch all day until it was late at night and then I'd go inside, try to shower if I felt like I could and then go to bed. As soon as I woke up, I'd make coffee and go right back outside.

This is how narcissistic and emotional abuse affected me.

How did this happen to the "life of the party," as I'd once thought of myself? The outgoing, no one could tell me, anything person?

I realized I was compartmentalizing the things that were happening to me because they were too hard for me to accept. To deal with. To control.

The best way I can describe this is I have files in my brain and although I'm aware of the situation, I would file them away until I absolutely needed them.

I slowly started referring back to what I like to call the "WTF" files and it became extremely hard for me to accept.

I'm writing this book to go through the "files" and explain how trauma affected me and how I'm working through it. Each chapter is a file, if you will and the more I write, the more I realize how many files I'd created during this time.

They will not be in perfect order because of the trauma. I'll remember things out of order. This book is my therapy and me being able to overcome what happened to me. I will never understand and that's something I've accepted. Overcoming is the goal. Educating others is the goal.

I will not let this event, this small portion of my life, dictate my happiness and well-being anymore. I'm a survivor and I'm a fighter. I am proud of myself!

Charming

Charming. That's what my husband was. He'd send me songs, bring home flowers just because, and take care of me when I was sick. He was always there for me.

He was the kind of man that would let me hug him for as long as I needed to. The kind of man that would cook dinner and fix my plate and bring it to me. He'd record us shows to watch together. He made me laugh. A thoughtful man.

He would clean and take care of maintenance on the home. He took the garbage out. He did all the things. I was happy with him. The day we went to the police station was when that changed. Everything changed. I still don't know why.

He always made me feel safe and secure. He's tall and has beautiful blue eyes and brownish hair. Handsome. I didn't doubt that he loved me. He showed me by being there and listening to me. He didn't need to say it; he showed me with acts of kindness and thoughtful gifts.

He was great with his kids. He made homemade birthday cakes for all of us, including coworkers. He loves to cook. He always popped fireworks for all the kids every holiday. He put the time in with everyone who was special to him. He was helpful. I need people to know this about him so that you can understand why I'm so confused and hurt by my situation.

How could someone who made me feel safe, make me feel so unsafe at the same time? It was weird. It was traumatic. I've formed a trauma bond with him. I miss him most days. But I get confused about what it is I miss. I miss the comfort of having him with me. The security he brought to my life. So to think there's a possibility that he helped do this to me is extremely hard to process. How can I? I tried therapy. It was informative and helped me see it wasn't healthy, but the feelings are still there.

I spoke to my psychiatrist, who explained gas lighting and narcissistic abuse. It was like they were talking about someone else. Not him. Not my life with him. I couldn't wrap my brain around the idea that he was lying to me, manipulating me.

As I said, he showed me how much he cared. What he didn't show me was how much he didn't. And that's the part I have to accept. Accepting the words of strangers over my husband felt like a betrayal. It felt wrong. I wanted it to be wrong. I didn't want a divorce. It took me sitting on the back porch in silence and paying attention and listening to realize that he was actually starting to fit the picture that's been painted of him.

Once I love someone, I will always love that person. It's how my heart works. I can't just make it go away. I maintain contact with everyone I've ever loved. It's always been important to me to part on good terms. We still talk. I know, I know. How can I write these things and still communicate with him? I don't know. It's that simple. I don't know. I'm emotionally damaged by the situation.

I guess my point is it's okay if you're going through something like this and you're confused. It's ok to feel protective of that person and also be angry at the same time because you do know the facts. The process of healing is slow. It's a journey. I'm still processing and he's still charming.

Agree To Disagree

This is a sensitive topic for me. My husband had two children from a previous marriage. I started dating my husband while he was going through his divorce. I know, frowned upon. But it's what happened.

I remember reading their agreement and thinking, this is absurd. I didn't understand why he agreed to everything. Money was a factor.

Once married, it really became a factor for me because we had the kids 50% of the time. Every four days we had off work; the kids were with us four days. So the need for child support and also the amount paid was always a question for me.

Alabama has a calculator where you can enter both parents' income and who pays for insurance and it'll total the cost for you. Simple.

But even without claiming the income the ex was making, he was still overpaying. And remember, we had them every 4 days for 4 days. We had to buy clothes and shoes and uniforms and pay medical bills, health insurance and all the extracurricular activities the children were involved in.

My husband was fine with that. I was not. His paycheck paid the mortgage and child support. I paid for everything else. So I started to become resentful that my money went towards all the other things when he overpaid child support and she didn't claim her income. From my understanding, she did pretty well. Always had a new vehicle. Nice home. I worked shift work and shift work is hard. Why did I have to pay for things she should be buying with the money we already gave?

This was a huge problem in my marriage. I brought it up all the time. Because we had the children as often as she and we had to supply a whole wardrobe and bedrooms. Which is fine, except why have to pay her anything?

He, as I said, didn't have an issue with it. But I'd have to work overtime anytime anyone needed anything extra. I had a problem with this and it wasn't going away.

After 9 years, he decided during this situation to take her to court. The police already told me there was an argument and secret conversations between them about custody. Why was it a secret? We had them all the time and did whatever the ex wanted. If she asked, she got it.

My husband insisted on this being the time to deal with a matter I'd been trying to deal with for nine years during a time I was dealing with identity theft. Didn't make sense. Noted.

I paid the attorney. Six thousand dollars. Me. I paid for it. He would tell me this is what I insisted on, but see, I'd given up years prior. I'd been told by the police they were arguing, so it wasn't me pushing the issue. But when my husband is angry, I give in. I gave him the money. Money I shouldn't have had to pay.

He never told me they went to court or that they agreed on anything. He did share with me the discovery papers her attorney requested because the things they were requesting were things about ME!

They wanted specific things. My 2018 1095, how much jewelry I own and the value, my clothes, and anything turned in to the police regarding my identity theft case. Crazy right? How did this affect a child support payment? They don't factor in the step-parent's income in Alabama and if they were at that point, well, she wasn't claiming hers nor her husband's.

I told my husband that considering she already had all of my personal information in her email, I would not be providing anything she requested and unless I was subpoenaed, they could kiss my ass. I also let him know that if I find out he does without my permission, I will sue him personally for volunteering private information about me to her of all people!

Nothing was mentioned to me about the status of the case or when the hearing would be or if one at all. I was told after the fact months later.

What I didn't know is that when they did settle, she was pregnant at the time and he handed over their settlement papers to me. I was shocked for one that he settled without discussing anything with me and it cost me six thousand dollars.

I scanned the papers because I'm not much of a reader and noticed some odd amendments to their original agreement. The children could not go by any last name other than what's on the birth certificate. They divorced ten years prior; why would that be added? Remember she was pregnant and I didn't know.

I found a binder in my husband's closet one day while hanging up his clothes and it was labeled custody. I wanted to know why it was so thick. Did he provide my information? I told him not to. He did. Inside was my 2018 1095, the Alexa analytic report I'd been trying to obtain but still couldn't access the account. How did he have that? And why was it part of custody? And why watch me stress beyond belief trying to access these accounts and not sharing what he had with me on MY accounts?!

I took pictures. The Alexa analytic report proved her dropping in the day I was in the bathroom. I was relieved to see that. The 1095 was weird. One of the things I hadn't mentioned yet was that all insurance, BCBS, Aflac, Teledoc, CVS and Walgreens all looked like I had two accounts. The ex-wife was on the CVS account, so she had access to see all of my prescriptions. Her email was attached to my Teledoc account as well. How is this legal?! And why was my 1095 important? I was on my husband's family insurance. I didn't pay for insurance. Except according to that 1095, I did!

I contacted my employer because my husband and I worked at the same place and well they owed me money. I explained what was going on and wanted them to look into it. They responded with Talk to your husband. Ok, except my husband didn't pay for Aflac; I did. It was my 1095 and my paystubs showing I was paying double. They've yet to this very day looked into that or cut me a check even though I provided all paystubs proving what I was saying.

In June of 2021, I called the children's hospital billing department like I had done for nine years and asked for a copy of the form to submit to my

Aflac for my stepdaughter. I have a legal right to do so. I've already looked up the law on that. The billing department said they needed to wait on Medicaid to pay it. What?!

She didn't have Medicaid; we all had BCBS. I immediately told my husband his ex is committing fraud and that something would need to be done because we were paying for health insurance. I already suspected she was scamming the food stamp office because the children were getting free breakfast and lunch at school. Between both parents and step-parents, we made enough money to provide. So why all the free stuff?

The ex-wife then, of course, knowing I was upset because my husband informed her of everything, called our BCBS and they provided her with information on OUR policy. But, I get told, talk to your husband. This infuriated me. Being an analytical thinker/investigator, I decided to read the policy for BCBS of AL. I discovered that they do not have the right to discuss the policy info, even if it's her child on the account, unless she's on the policy. I called BCBS and was told, you guessed it, to talk to my husband. What do they think he knows? What don't I know?! I'm so confused!

Of course, he didn't know anything. He didn't understand why every company from A-Z was telling me to talk to my husband. What in the hell was he doing? What were they doing?

The police told me to quit digging for information for safety reasons. The less I knew, the safer I'd be. Well, how does one do that when their life is upside down and full of questions?

And who's the father of the unborn baby? Because the child support was not lowered at all. In fact, they took his time away, so instead of every four days of having them for four days, it was now every other weekend. Interesting. Noted.

I made it my business to write about this because it did concern me. I'm part of the discovery. I paid the attorney. I have a right to know. And honestly, I feel if she can make my life hers... well, you get the point.

Inside Out

Will It Matter When You're Eighty?

Inside out, outside in. The body always keeps the score. In March of 2021, I started losing weight. I wasn't sure why. I wasn't mad about it. I was a little overweight at the time, not much, but I could have stood to lose a few pounds.

I noticed I couldn't swallow like I used to; everything was kind of getting stuck on the right side of my throat. Every time I'd swallow, I'd have to do an extra gulp just to get all of my food down. I then started noticing the uncomfortableness after I ate. Well, before I knew it, I was only eating once a day, and I would eat at night right before bed so that I wouldn't have to deal with the discomfort that came after I ate a meal.

I was dealing with excessive burping, bloating and pain, especially in the center of my chest, right between my breast bone. I would have pain that would radiate all the way around my back. Not to mention that I started choking on my food at this point. Not long after, the weight loss was noticeable to other people. I started getting compliments. Hey, you look great!! I admit, I loved those compliments! Who wouldn't?

Fast forward a few months and I was now getting told I needed to eat a cheeseburger, that I was too skinny and my jeans were sagging. What was wrong with me? Well, the body keeps the score, see, and I was dealing with a tremendous amount of stress. Stress that I don't even know how I've survived. Stress that I had to compartmentalize just to make it through.

That wasn't the only health concern I had at the time. At this point, I had lost sixty pounds without trying. Sixty. That's a lot for someone who's 5'3". At my lowest point, I was down to 102 pounds. I hadn't weighed under 120 since middle school. I was grossly skinny, in my opinion. To look at myself in the mirror, I did not recognize who this person was. I could see every bone in my body.

I had a lot of muscle waste. I was in a size zero. I was a size eight prior. That's a lot. But my other health concern started a few months prior to the weight loss. I had developed nodules on my legs all the way from my ankle to my hips.

They kind of looked like sores or blisters, and they were perfectly round, about the size of a pencil eraser. There were hundreds of them. I would wear jeans all the time, or pants to work, so no one had to see them. I didn't want anyone to know. Summer was approaching, shorts season, where you would want to wear shorts or dresses, and I wouldn't because I didn't want anybody to know what was going on with my skin. I didn't know what was going on with my skin or why this was happening. I had still yet to see a doctor about the weight loss because, to be honest with you, I wasn't that mad about it.

Yeah, I didn't enjoy choking on my food or being in pain after I ate, but I'd always had upper GI problems. I had a history of ulcers, so I just assumed, okay, well, I must have a few stomach ulcers. I'm under a tremendous amount of stress. So I justified it. And I didn't seek physician treatment. But the legs. The legs bothered me. The legs were where I said, okay, enough's enough. And I sought out a dermatologist.

It was during COVID, so they only offered video appointments, and I showed her my body. She wanted to see everything. And I showed her. It was just on my limbs. I had a few on my back, but not many. Not like my legs. She immediately said, it's Prurigo nodularis, and I thought, huh? What is Prurigo nodularis? I'd never even heard that. I'm pretty sure I didn't even pronounce that correctly the first time she told me. I had to ask her to spell it.

She explained to me she would call in some cream and some ointment because several of the spots looked infected and that she wanted to see me in the office in two weeks for a biopsy. Well, that scared me. I've had biopsies before. I've had moles removed. I'd been told before, because of my skin type, I'm olive skin, that I would need to see a dermatologist regularly. People that have darker skin, which I don't know if you guys know this or not, but if you have darker skin, you actually need to be seen more because you can withstand the sun for longer periods of time than someone who does not have your skin tone. So actually, you need to be getting your skin checked regularly.

Of course, me being the non-compliant person that I am and the person that likes to justify everything and explain everything away, didn't go back. I didn't go for the biopsy.

In September 2021, my dad called. He was living in Tennessee at the time, and he told me if I did not go to the doctor that, he would drive down from Tennessee. Now, I'm 39 years old, so I don't know why that bothered me in any way because I mean, I'm 39, and he can't tell me what to do. But I guess his concerns sparked concern in me. So I made an appointment with the GI doctor (gastroenterologist) because, like I said, I figured I had ulcers. I've had them before. I figured that's what it was. I go to a new doctor because my old doctor knew my medical history and with the leg thing going on, well, I didn't want him to know.

I wore jeans that day to my appointment. I didn't fill my paperwork out all the way. No medical history, no family medical history. I didn't want him to know anything. So I listed a few of my symptoms. As soon as he walked into the room, I could tell he was looking me up and down. Doctors do this. It didn't phase me much but most of them are very casual about it, and they're checking you out head to toe without you even noticing. But this doctor, it was very noticeable.

He asked me what all my symptoms were. I explained that I was having some dysphagia, which is difficulty swallowing. I explained that I had discomfort in the center right between my breast bone that extended around to my back. He asked for me to lie down on the exam table because he wanted to do an abdominal exam, palpate or whatever they call it.

He felt around for a good ten minutes. I noticed how thorough he was with this examination. And I thought, okay, this is the longest that I've ever had to endure this. I've had people feel on my stomach before. What is he feeling? He asked me to sit up and he said to me, "What else is going on?" And I smiled, he said, "What aren't you telling me?" And he saw my ankle. Great. I didn't want anyone to know. My ankle had a "sore" on it or a nodule. He asked me to pull my pants legs up. Well, I'm still in the skinny jean phase, so I barely pulled them up because I can barely get them to pull up. And he looked me dead in my eyes and said, "I think that you have cancer or an autoimmune disorder. It's one of the two. It can only be one of the two. So what is it?"

"Well, I mean, I don't know," I replied. "Shouldn't you have someone come with me and hold my hand before you say something like that to someone?" I'm very nonchalant about things with a dark sense of humor and was very unemotional at the time. Anyway, he explained to me the seriousness of the situation, the amount of weight loss that I had combined with the symptoms I was having indicated something very serious. Had I seen anyone about my legs? "Oh, yes, saw a dermatologist, I answered. They want me to get a biopsy." He asked, "Did you get the biopsy?" I said, "No, should I?" He replied, "Hell yes, you need the biopsy! We need to know what is going on with you. Do you not understand that I think that you have cancer?!" "Okay, well, I mean, I guess if you think that I really need to go do it," I said. "Is it work or home?" he replied. "What do you mean?" I replied. "Stress. Is it work, or is it home?" he asked again.

Well, I started to get emotional. I wasn't there to see the GI doctor to talk about work or home. So as I was tearing up and trying to hold them in, I replied, both. It's both. He rolled the little stool over and looked me dead in my eyes again. And he says to me, "Is it going to matter when you're 80?" Well, I didn't understand what he meant by that at the time. I did not understand at all. I just kind of shrugged my shoulders and thought, oh. Well, he says to me, "I'm going to put you through a series of tests. We're going to figure out what this is. Don't worry. I've got you."

Okay. I don't know how I was supposed to be feeling because the only thing I felt was upset that he had asked me about work or home. I didn't hear anything that he said about my health, like at all. I heard him, but it didn't register. I didn't take it seriously. It didn't scare me. I didn't have any feelings at all about it. I just didn't care. After having lab work done, I left. And, of course, all the phone calls come in from my friends, my family and my husband. They all wanted to know what the doctor said.

I told everyone just like he said it. Oh, well, he thinks I might have cancer or an autoimmune disorder. And silence from everyone. "Oh, I'm so sorry, Brooke. You're going to be okay." And I'm thinking, I'm fine. What are you talking about? I'm completely fine. I'm not worried at all. I don't understand why you have all this concern. I'm totally fine.

The doctor gets the lab work results and well, the lab work isn't good. My eosinophils, neutrophils and monocytes were high. I had immature granulocytes. Usually, people don't have immature granulocytes unless they have cancer or they're in their third trimester of pregnancy, according to Google. My red blood cell count, white blood cell count and red blood cell distribution width weren't looking good. Okay, the lab results were horrible.

The next test was an abdominal ultrasound. I go in for the test. I've had these before. I have a history of ulcers. So this is the first test they do insurance based. I go in and the tech is talking to me and she is trying to distract me from looking at the screen. She was very quick. And I thought, wow, this is the easiest ultrasound I've ever had of my abdomen. I mean, I was in there less than ten minutes, and she was done. I thought immediately, okay, she's found something. Once she was done, she escorted me out. She explained she would get the results off to the radiologist and let him read them and then they would get back to me. But I felt hurried out of the room. I knew something was wrong.

That was unnerving for me. It takes about ten minutes for me to get home from the hospital. Within that ten-minute timeframe, on the app that they let you access your results from, I got a notification. The results were in. That quick. I panicked. My pancreas was decreased but also showed edema. So I immediately went back to my lab work because I knew that that could be pancreatitis if my lab work for my pancreas was off. It was not. So the only alternative to that would've been pancreatic cancer. Well, I don't really know the statistics on that, but I did know that Patrick Swayze and Alex Trebek had pancreatic cancer. And they didn't live long. I started crying. At that moment, I think I realized, oh shit, something is seriously wrong with me.

I didn't wait to hear back from the doctor. I didn't need to. The radiologist read the report. I read my labs, and put two and two together. I had pancreatic cancer. That's my diagnosis. That's what I had convinced myself of. After about fifteen minutes of freaking out, I call Leslie. She's an RN. I'm matter-of-factly telling her this information. Unemotional, just here are the results. What do you think? And she didn't know what to say either because we both knew it wasn't good. And it was an ultrasound. Ultrasounds aren't supposed to be as good as an MRI or a CT. So if it was showing up like this on an ultrasound, well, God forbid, I go get the

CT and MRI, I mean, what's that going to show? Right? The doctor's office called and didn't say anything to me about what the ultrasound results were.

They just said we've ordered an abdominal CT for you now with contrast. Okay??? Well, guess what? My pancreas was fine on the CT, thank God, but guess what wasn't? My liver. My liver was not okay. They found a lesion on my liver. What kind of lesion? They didn't know. They assumed it could be a hemangioma. It was very small. My liver was enlarged, but everything else seemed to look really good.

The next journey in my health was another foot fracture. I haven't talked about my health much in the book, but in August of 2021, I broke two bones in my foot. I broke a metatarsal and I broke a pinky toe by just jamming my foot into the end of an end table. That's all it took. And they broke.

Fast forward to October and it happened again on the other foot. This time I felt the bones break. I knew which bones were broken. I'd also been experiencing severe shoulder pain. I knew that I couldn't reach back very far. I couldn't put my seatbelt on with my left arm. I couldn't pick my arm up far enough to lean back to wash my hair in the shower. It was like my shoulder would get stuck out of place. It was very odd.

I made an appointment with an orthopedic doctor. I go in to have him assess my shoulder and my broken foot. He wants x-rays and decides that he wants an MRI of not only my shoulder but also my back. Okay, so GI doctor, pause. Orthopedic, you're up. I get the MRI for both the shoulder and the back.

I go back in for the results and I'm told that I have bone spurs in my shoulder that have caused a tear in my rotator cuff. I'm only 39 years old, so why do I have bone spurs? Well, the doctor thought that too. He also thought it was very odd that I was able to tell him before he did an x-ray on my foot which bones were broken. I was very specific; it's my fifth metatarsal and my pinky toe. He thought I was insane. He said, let's just get the X-ray. Let's make sure. Well, sure enough, I was correct. That was very disturbing to him. How did I know which bones I had broken? Most people don't even know if they break a bone, right?

After the MRI of the shoulder and back, he determines that I need not only shoulder surgery but back surgery as well. At this point, I'd been referred to a hematologist oncologist because of my lab work. So he instructed me to notify the hematologist-oncologist that I have bone spurs and I've had multiple fractures within a year. At this point, I think I was at my fourth fracture very easily.

I go see the hematologist oncologist and she sends me to the lab for more extensive bloodwork. She told me she thinks that I have Waldenstrom's syndrome or scleroderma, but to be sure, she wants to send me to a rheumatologist. Okay, let's go see the rheumatologist. The rheumatologist says, very quickly after looking at me, I do not have scleroderma. He had no comment on Waldenstrom's because I was there to rule out scleroderma.

Do I have the Waldenstroms? Well, I don't know. Because from what I've researched and understand is that it would require a bone marrow biopsy to diagnose. I got referred to a neurologist because I was continuing to fall. Loss of balance, I assumed, just because I had broken both pinky toes and metatarsals on both feet. So naturally, I should have a loss of balance, correct? Here I go justifying everything. Now, my right eye is drooping and my mouth on the right side of my face noticeably.

The neurologist asked me if I had ever had Botox. Well, me being me, not taking things very seriously, I'm flattered by the question. I was like, oh, well, no, not me. I haven't had Botox. I'm blushing while saying this. This is just what I look like. And I kind of giggled, and I thought it was cute.

Well, it wasn't cute because the problem was that he could tell that part of my face was paralyzed to some degree. I heard him out in the hall yelling at the nurses. She needs an MRI of her brain stat! This was right before Christmas of 2021. At this point, they could not get me in anywhere. They called all the hospitals. They had an MRI machine in their building, but they could not get me in. This was on a Friday. I was scheduled the following Monday for an MRI of the brain by my primary physician. He opted to just keep that appointment, although he thought I might be having a TIA or a mini-stroke while I was in his office. So it wasn't cute anymore.

I go for the MRI of the brain and everything checks out. Everything looks good. No MS, no lesions on the brain, which I have two family members that have had brain tumors. None. They don't see anything wrong. Everything checks out fine. I had a carotid ultrasound. I was told the results of that were fine, although they suspected something was wrong there. So this is all very odd, right? And I'm getting tired of going to the doctors. I think at this point I had eight physicians. I did finally get the skin biopsy from the dermatologist. She took one off of each thigh, and it came back as lichen simplex chronicus, which basically said cancer or autoimmune. So all of my results up until this point were still indicating the same thing. Cancer, autoimmune, cancer or autoimmune. Well, I will say that the hematologist oncologist gave two definitive diagnoses.

One of them was granulacytosis, which is basically abnormal lab work. The other diagnosis was called osler hemorrhagic telangiectasia syndrome (Osler HHT), which is a hereditary disorder that my grandmother had. I was told by my GI doctor to start referring back, going through all my medical history, going back through all of my family medical histories, asking all the questions, get all of the records. So I did. I was starting to take things seriously. And to be honest, it was an escape from the identity theft.

I was able to retrieve everything up until 2015. And what I discovered is that my labs had always looked like that. They were never right. Specifically in 2020 when I had back surgery. My labs looked like I was a leukemia patient. The surgeon decided to move forward with my surgery. And not only did he move forward with my surgery, but when he got in to do the surgery, he found, in his words, an abundance of vascular lesions. Well, that's interesting, considering that I just got the Osler HHT diagnosis and that they thought that the lesion on my liver was a hemangioma.

So what does this all mean? Well, I don't know. You tell me. Because they haven't still to this date and it's now December 2022, I do not know. I've had multiple abdominal ultrasounds and multiple abdominal CTs. Consistently they show enlarged liver, getting bigger lesions, now multiple lesions, and they don't know what they are. I've had an EGD and a colonoscopy where they took eight biopsies, but I was told they were fine. So what is going on with my body? I don't know. Is it stress?

I asked the hematologist-oncologist that question, and she said, well, yes, it could be. Stress does weird things to the body. Had I been stressed since 2015? Her recommendation to me was for me to go, and, in quotes, "somewhere bigger." She did not refer me to anyone.

She just told me to go somewhere bigger because the type of tumor that my mom, my sister and my grandmother had was nothing that she was familiar with. I would need to go somewhere bigger to get this diagnosed. My GI doctor, who promised me that we would get to the bottom of this, wants to send me to the Mayo Clinic. He made that decision back in August. It's December of 2022, and I have yet to be referred to the Mayo Clinic.

So what is going on and why does it take so long? Let's just all hope for their sake and mine that it's not something very serious. The whole point is the body keeps the score. What was going on inside my body was now showing on the outside. Is what happened to me why my body was failing me? I don't know. It's been going on for so long that who can keep the score anymore?

Will it matter when I'm eighty? The goal is to make it to eighty. I get it now. I can't be stressed. What I see on the outside is coming from the inside.

Leaving Sprinkles

While waiting on the results of all the scans from the doctors and waiting to find out if I had a potentially life-threatening disease, I decided to do a do-it-yourself autobiography.

I was always such a private person and there were several things in my life I'd never discussed with anyone or feelings I'd shared.

I wanted to leave a book behind for the people that love me. To share my thoughts on life and my life as I knew it. I don't have children to tell my story and pass on, so for me; it was my way of leaving something behind.

My sister and I both have a dark sense of humor, so during that particular time in my life, she was the only one that I could talk to about my wishes after my death. The book actually asks you those questions and I felt like I had to prepare for it. I looked sick and I felt sick. I just wanted someone to know my feelings.

She would entertain everything I said and even help come up with ideas for my wake and funeral. We'd laugh and joke about all the different things we'd plan. It was, in a weird way, an escape for me. From the reality of my situation.

I won't go into details about what we talked about, but just know that I enjoyed having my sister, especially during those moments. I appreciated all the belly laughs and snorts that came with it and felt at ease knowing that she'd handle everything in the way I wanted. Nothing too serious, just a touch of me for all those that loved me and a good laugh.

The book starts with your early childhood and ends with the present time in your life. I found myself unable to complete certain parts. I still had things I wanted to do! Places I wanted to go! I started the book in December of 2021 and as my fortieth birthday was approaching, I felt the need to make a bucket list.

I had to name it my forties bucket list for my mom's sake, but when I created it, I knew what kind of list I was making. I wanted to do things I'd never done before, like riding in a hot air balloon, parasailing and zip lining. I didn't feel these were too much to ask until I started asking friends to go with me. Not one person felt brave enough to commit. I still laugh at that to this day. A bunch of chickens!

Eventually, without answers from the doctors and me starting to slowly gain weight again, the list did actually convert to the forties bucket list. I'm determined to cross things off before I'm fifty.

I've always thought about the different roles we play in others' lives. How we affect them, good, bad, or changed.

I call it leaving sprinkles. I've always tried to leave sprinkles along the way with everyone I encounter. Whether it's a smile to someone who's not smiling, a hug when someone hasn't felt a human touch in a while, a word of encouragement when someone needs to hear it, a listening ear when someone just needs to be heard, a "how are you" when no one's asked in a while or compliment to make them feel special.

I'm sure I've hurt people. I know I've said things that have left people feeling less than good. I'm not proud of that and I'm not perfect. I have good days and bad days, just like everyone. Sometimes I'm the one that needs to be on the receiving end.

I want to be remembered for making people feel good and better for being around me. I want to leave a good impression everywhere I go. A legacy, if you will.

I never want to leave anyone wondering how I feel about them or make them feel bad about themselves. It's important for me to be impactful. My situation, in some ways, has changed me for the better. I've opened up more, and my relationships with friends and family have grown stronger. I say what's on my mind instead of bottling it up.

I've gotten used to saying I love you to all of my family and friends after every phone call. Or hugging them bye when they leave. I answer the phone when it rings. There was a time in my life that I didn't do these things. I was so guarded and the walls were so high that no one could approach me.

I'm thankful for the change it forced me to make. A change for the better. I'm proud of myself for not completely shutting down and closing everyone out. I instead did the opposite and tried my best not to let what happened to me define me.

I am not what happened to me! I am much more. I often listen to a Chris Cornell song called "I Am The Highway." I love the lyrics. The meaning behind them and how they remind me that I am so much more than what anyone thinks of me or how they treat me. It's a reminder of how great I am.

My wish is for everyone to feel that way. Empowered and hopeful. I don't want to put up with less than I deserve anymore. Life is short and we should get what we give or at least have people in our lives that can give us what we are lacking at the moment and build us back up.

We should bring out the best in each other and anyone that wants to tear me down is no longer welcomed in my life. I've found my value. I've spent the majority of my life feeling the need for validation from others. I can validate myself. I can love myself. There are moments when I find myself still looking for that in others, but it's a process. No one changes overnight, but I know I'm headed in the right direction. I've grown.

I hope you all take something from this and choose to leave sprinkles along the way. The world needs it more than we even know.

Two Houses

What home?

In 2016 my ex-mother-in-law passed away. This was my first husband's mother. She was one of the sweetest people I've ever known.

We had a very close relationship even after the divorce from her son. She congratulated me when I remarried. It was a few short months after I remarried that she passed. A few years prior, she wrote a will. I was there when she wrote it. I knew exactly what it said.

In 2012 she purchased a home with cash for her son and me. We separated not long after, but I'd invested a lot of money into the home, but the home wasn't mine technically.

In her will, with one sentence in black and white, she wrote the property goes to her son and me and that the estate would cover any costs as far as property tax, etc.

When she passed, I waited to be notified of the will, but I never received word. Her sister was the executor and knew how to reach me. Four months after her passing, her sister reached out but not to notify me of the will. Instead, she notified me that they would foreclose on the home I hadn't lived in since 2013 if I didn't pay them for the house. Huh? Confused right?! Me too.

How can you foreclose on a property that has no mortgage and you're currently renting out? It made no sense. I asked for a copy of the will to which she never responded. I then contacted the attorney that was over the estate and asked for a copy, only to find out that the will was already probated. Someone had forged my name. I'm seeing a trend here.

The attorney eventually mailed a copy of the will to me and there it was, in black and white, the one sentence stating very clearly that the property now belonged to her son and I. I sought legal advice and no one could understand how they could foreclose on something that is owned outright and well, neither did I. No one wanted to take the case. I was on my own. My husband didn't feel like I should fight it because it would tie me to my ex.

I didn't give up. They tried to list the home for sale in 2017 and I contacted the realtor and explained the situation and it was taken off the market immediately. The executor then rented out the home and I never gave permission nor received funds from this.

Fast forward to September 2021. Yep. That many years later and I'm served with papers suing me for the full cost of the home. Just me. I immediately sought counsel. This time someone listened and we were going after them!

We filed a motion to have the executor removed due to them not fulfilling their duties. We found out that my ex-husband signed a paper without knowing, giving his portion of the home to his grandfather, who is now deceased. Now it's me against the executor.

I was awarded my half in court, along with half of the rent that should've been collected. They ordered an appraisal of the property only to find out that the persons living there were making a claim on the property as well. They were claiming they were renting to own. What?! This is all occurring in the middle of everything else I'm going through.

When I found out who was living there, I was even more shocked. It was my current sister-in-law and her boyfriend!! I know! I can't make this up! It's now February 2023 and we are still waiting for them to be evicted. I don't understand why things turn out the way they do, but I hope one day someone will honor my sweet mother-in-law's will and I'll be given what I was meant to have. Until then, nothing. Still.

Living in the '90s

Remember when you had to have conversations in person, for the most part? Not everyone had a cellphone and the ones that did, didn't have internet. The era of AOL dial-up computers. No debit cards really, just checks and cash. Cash would help in negotiating...

Well, for me, I lived that way for almost two years. My cellphone wouldn't let me access the internet. I couldn't access my bank account, so the bank wouldn't let me have a debit card. I had to drive to the bank and write a check for cash anytime I needed to buy anything. No more online shopping. And most places don't even accept cash anymore. Crazy huh?

My friends didn't want me calling or texting their phones because they experienced problems after I'd call. We could hear others' conversations while on the phone at times. So for the better part of a year, my main source of communication was in person. Which, to be honest, wasn't that bad. It was nice to look at the person you were talking to, but also very upsetting when you needed to talk to them right then. Or when most of your family lives out of state.

Because of the issues with my phone, email, and other accounts, I wasn't able to dial certain numbers or receive calls from certain numbers. The messed up part, as if that wasn't enough, is that my doctors weren't even able to get in touch with me to discuss my tests and scans. The hospital couldn't call me to schedule the testing I needed. This interferes with my healthcare. My well-being, both mentally and physically.

In the age of technology, could you imagine going backward? It took a very strong will not to get angry. I was determined not to let this situation defeat me. I instead chose to write, paint and watch the sunset every day. I'm so proud of myself for that. Kids these days will freak out if you take anything electronic away. I had everything taken away like I was on restriction for a long period of time.

The only thing I wanted to revisit in the 90s was the music and social interactions. When we made time to drive five minutes to see our friends instead of a phone call or FaceTime.

That was another thing I couldn't do. FaceTime. My mom and I would Facetime daily for hours until this happened. We weren't able to talk to each other for 5 months. She ended up with Covid and was in the ICU and I never knew.

I didn't get to speak to her on my birthday. My 40th birthday. My first birthday I didn't hear her voice singing Happy Birthday To You!

Halloween and Playing Postman

On this particular Halloween of 2021, I was sitting on the back porch where I'd been camping out for four months at the time. I always sit in the same spot. I never move.

However, for whatever reason, on this gorgeous day at almost sunset, I decided to go into the yard and sit on the swing. I was on the phone with Leslie and I noticed something. We had a privacy fence, so you really couldn't see in or out, but for some reason, I could see that day, through the fence.

I noticed a vehicle parked in the front of my house, more to the side, so our ring doorbell wouldn't pick it up. How clever. It's as if this hadn't been the first time. I noticed the vehicle had been there for a minute. So I decided to go check it out. After all, I didn't have anything better to do. It wasn't like my husband invited me to go trick or treating with him and his children. So I had nothing but time.

As I open the gate, I noticed a casually dressed female with brownish hair and glasses in my mailbox. What? Right. In my mailbox. I did have mail frequently missing at this point. Now I immediately recognized this person. She was what I like to call, well, a damn stalker. It was the ex-wife.

I yelled, "What are you doing" while still on the phone. She never looked at me. Why would she? She knew she was in trouble. I'd caught her red-handed, committing a felony. She quickly got in her car. The funny part about this is we lived on a corner lot. The neighborhood had one way in and one way out. She would need to drive past me to get out. I can't help but laugh at the idea she thought she wouldn't have to look at me.

I approached the side of my yard where she would be passing and I put my hands up in a what are you doing type stance. She slammed on the brakes and angrily rolled down her window. Why was she angry?! Um, my bad. Am I disturbing her? Is what I thought. Ha! She had the nerve to immediately start yelling at me. I have to admit I went deaf at that moment and saw color. Red, to be exact. I saw red. The entire time Leslie was still on the phone.

How is it that someone is in my mailbox and now yelling at me? Well, I let her know very quickly she was not only not allowed on my property ever again but also not anywhere with Bluetooth connection capability.

It was then she said I would not be allowed around her children. Huh? Because she stole my mail? She explained her children could not be at my home if I was there. She then sped off.

Now the funny part is, well, it was Halloween. She was playing Postman. She could've done a better job with the outfit if you ask me, but I'm not usually one to judge.

I returned to my conversation with Leslie, who was now already on her way to my house because she partially heard the exchange of words. I assured her I wouldn't need her assistance, but her concern was not about the ex-wife but my husband.

I hadn't even thought of that. And boy, was she right! He immediately came outside while on the phone with the ex-asking me, what did you do?!

He then ends his call and asks me what happened. I explained the whole situation and reminded him that the day prior I had asked him to put an end to her coming to our home unannounced. The day prior to this, she'd shown up and dropped off clothes for the girls on our front porch with no one knowing.

This is odd for several reasons. She never came to our house. She was privileged in that way because whatever she needed, my husband would do. When she did come by, which was very, very seldom, she never got out of the car. So why now have I seen her so many times in such a short period? And why did she insist on coming all the way to the door?

It wasn't long after the incident that I texted her. She had mentioned receiving my mail at her home. That's even more odd. So she's in my mailbox and receiving my mail at her home? Hmmm. I asked her why she didn't deliver my mail when she came by the previous day and she explained that when she opened it, I know she opened my mail, that it was medical forms that she had returned to Urgent Care and that I could contact them to retrieve that.

So just to be clear and I'm no expert on law, but accessing someone's mailbox, now receiving mail and opening it that contains medical forms, is not being looked at as an issue by the police? That's not right, is it? I immediately contacted the Inspector General and reported the incident and attached screenshots of the text thread of her admitting to what she did.

I never heard a word back. Why? Well, I was hacked. I barely received any phone calls. Of course, I didn't hear anything. I went to my local post office and explained the incident, where I was advised to contact the local police department. I laughed so hard. Why would I contact them?! They weren't helping at all! I, however emailed the detectives anyway and received no response.

I'd asked prior to this for a restraining order against her and was told it was still under investigation. This could've been prevented. I still, to this day, have no such order of protection from someone I can prove has committed multiple felonies in accordance with Alabama state law.

Throughout this situation, I continued to report, document and take action. No one has helped me. I don't know if they don't know where to start or how... all I know is that I was alone in all the ways when it came to protecting myself against her actions.

The next day she texted my husband, expressing her concern for the kids and his safety around me. ME. The person that doesn't commit crimes. The person that sits on the back porch and minds their own business. If I don't laugh, I'll cry. That's how ridiculous this situation had become.

Any who, watch your mailbox, people. There's thieves out there.

Friends Along The Way

(You Win Some, You Lose Some)

It's hard to believe but I've had the same friend group since I was fifteen years old. Of course, I had a few new friends during that time, but my close friends were there for twenty-five years.

When this incident first occurred, I lost friends and I gained friends. Some will be lifetime friends, no doubt.

I'd reached out to Summer on "D Day," and her lack of understanding drove a wedge between us. It broke my heart. It was a misunderstanding, I guess. But I can only tell my side of what happened. She'd just lost her younger sister days before. She was upset and grieving at the time and understandably so. When I called her that day from my closet, whispering and hysterical, she told me to go to bed, that my husband was right and I needed sleep. She told me that she'd also been up all night and she was going to bed and would not be going to the birthday party.

I called Leslie after and while on the phone with her, she said, "Summer just walked up and is talking to your husband." What?! How is she there and not in bed? That's crazy, right?! I mean, the nerve. I was so angry at her. To me, it was like this, when she chose to leave her house that day she could've turned two ways, 1. She could've come to her hysterical, scared friend or 2. Go to my husband? Honestly, option two wasn't even something I would've ever thought of. So, I guess really there was only one answer there. You go to your friend!

I said some pretty hateful things to Summer that day. Why wouldn't I? She chose his side. This is what I'd thought. This is how it looked from my point of view. I told Summer never to speak to me again. And she didn't. For a year and a half. My best friend gone during the most difficult and confusing time of my life. I was so heartbroken over that. I'd tried apologizing multiple times to her from the many phones I'd acquired during that time and no response. Our friendship ended on "D Day."

Well, "D Day" changed a lot of friendships that day. Mine and Summer's, Mine and Kathy's, Lindsey and Kay's, my husband and Lindsey's husband. I refer to this as "The Great Divide." Why did this happen? Could it have been what I said that morning? "I know everything" to my husband? I think so. I'm sure of it.

There were so many changes in my life at that time. I made a new friend that is very dear to me. Her name is CJ. We met in the oddest way. I laugh thinking back on it because I contacted her and, to be honest, probably shouldn't have, but I'm so grateful I did. See, CJ is, and stay with me on this one, my husband's ex-wife's current husband's ex-wife. Lol! I know that sounds like drama city. Well, it was really.

When my husband and I were still communicating, we discovered in the oldest child's phone she had a contact programmed as "X." So I searched the number on the internet and found out it was CJ. Well, we wanted to know why the oldest kid was calling her stepdad's ex-wife. This was weird. And why was it a secret? Well, my husband made me do the dirty work, so I made the call.

I explained who I was and why I was concerned. CJ told me she'd never spoken to the oldest kid and was very confused, just like me! So I went into what was going on with our devices and she listened. She listened. My friend of twenty-five years didn't, but someone I didn't know was listening to me!

She's never stopped listening to me. We became fast friends and stay in touch to this day. CJ, thank you for being there for me even when you didn't understand what I was saying.

Dee. Dee was already in my circle of friends but not really a close friend of mine. Not yet, anyway. But one day, while at Lindsey's, Dee shows up. And it was interesting because she sat next to me and kept looking over at me as if I was a distraction to her conversation with Lindsey. After a few minutes of this, she took off her gloves and handed them to me. She just knew. She knew I was sick. And one of my symptoms were cold hands and feet. She never knew that prior. At that moment, I knew Dee was special. She was kind, she paid attention and she cared. I opened up to her that night about everything I'd been dealing with and she listened. For me, that's everything. People need to be heard. Dee was there several times for me during this situation. She's given me clothes to wear when I lost weight. She's brought me beer when my anxiety was bad. I know I've made a friend for life with her and although we don't talk often, when we do talk, it always has great depth.

Kathy. Kathy and I have a different kind of bond. We've known each other since we were sixteen, but we married cousins. My husband and her ex-husband are first cousins and we shared a last name and my stepdaughters and her youngest daughter were second cousins. We always had a lot to talk about when we would see each other at the friend gatherings, but we never really spoke outside of that.

Kathy or Kat as I call her, is always smiling. She can smile through an entire conversation while I'm making the weirdest faces! She's always pleasant to be around and naturally beautiful. She's a sweet soul and I don't know why we never got super close. When the identity theft occurred and the great divide happened, she distanced herself even more from me. She chose not to speak to me. She thought my situation was weird and didn't want anything to do with it. She was friends with Kay. They spent a lot of time together.

In a way, I felt betrayed by this, but why? We were never super close. I guess it was because we shared the same friend group and I had an expectation of her. I expected her to call me the day Kay showed up at her daughter's birthday party with my stepdaughters. That is not okay. Maybe I shouldn't have placed those expectations on her. I don't know. My feelings are my feelings and I felt hurt that she chose Kay over me and would speak about my situation, just not to me. She was close with Summer and Kay after the divide. We've since talked and we've never had a conversation concerning what happened that day. We've instead just picked up where we left off before the party. Kat often calls now and you can always hear her smile through the phone. She calls with words of encouragement and I'm grateful for that.

Amanda. Amanda is a beautiful soul. She's genuinely sweet. Amanda helped me out during a time I needed her most. Amanda owns her own business. She owns a cleaning business and she's phenomenal. When we were preparing to sell the house and getting it ready to show, I reached out to Amanda for help. I couldn't mop or scrub the bathtubs anymore because of my shoulder and back. I really didn't have money to pay her either. Without hesitation, she fit me into her extremely busy schedule and instead of sending someone who works for her to come help, she showed up. And she stayed for five hours deep cleaning the entire home. And she didn't charge me a dime. Amanda is kind. I love her too.

Mary Ann. Mary Ann was, at first, just my hair stylist. I was so embarrassed the first time I'd let her do my hair because it had been well over a year since I'd had it done. It was long and I needed highlights badly. To say I have tangles is an understatement. I'd opened up to Mary Ann and, at first, only shared about my health. I was grossly skinny at this point and it looked unnatural, so I felt I had to tell her, really. She listened. And was strong. Gave encouraging words and well, my hair looked fantastic.

Summer paid for me to have my hair done because I was unemployed and well my husband didn't provide for me after I lost my job. Mary Ann didn't even say anything when she noticed the name on the credit card. I think she knew I'd been through a lot. Throughout the last year and several kept hair appointments later, we've developed a friendship. I'm so happy to say she's my friend and made sure to give her the annual Christmas friend ornament. Thank you, Mary Ann, for everything.

Friendship is hard. You have to put the work in. You have to listen and show up! You have to believe the unbelievable. I'll admit I haven't always been the greatest friend. But I did learn from this situation and I have grown tremendously as a friend from it. These women have taught me what true friendship is. Leslie and Lindsey never left my side. They always showed up. They always listened. They always fed me. They took turns taking me to doctors' appointments. Two very remarkable women whom I admire greatly. But they are two different people.

Lindsey. Lindsey is the glue. She's the one who patches things up if there's been an argument amongst anyone in our friend circle. She's always first to address a situation. The first to apologize. She's the youngest of us all and yet the matriarch, if you will, of our friend family. She an excellent writer, conversationalist, and listener. She pays attention even when she hasn't a clue about what

I'm saying. She stays the course and doesn't give up until everything is right. She is strong and sensitive. She has big beautiful blue eyes and she's thoughtful. She's the friend that will not only drop off dinner for you but include an encouraging note along with it.

Leslie. Leslie is the light. When she walks into a room, always smiling ear to ear, you can literally see her glowing. She's so beautiful outside and in. She gives the best hugs and you can feel how much she loves you. Her heart is too big for her own good sometimes and I've tried to pour back into her what she gives to me. Leslie sent me daily devotionals during that time. She prayed with me. She visited me when she could. She brought beer; I know it's a trend... We've laughed together and cried together so many times throughout our friendship and I think we are the closest we've ever been. Leslie, you are truly an angel on Earth.

Summer is home. Summer is the friend I've had the longest. After a year and a half of not talking and several pushes from Lindsey to do so, we finally did. Summer didn't know anything that I was dealing with after July 24, 2021. She didn't know I was sick. She didn't know all the things I'd been dealing with in the identity theft situation. But this particular day, she listened to me. Finally! And she was very upset. From that moment forward, she switched into high gear and wanted to handle everything for me. She knew now how fragile I was physically, mentally, and emotionally.

She wanted to take it all on. She wanted to move me in with her so she could take care of me. Even though she was going to nursing school to further her degree, had a full-time job and was newly engaged. She didn't care. She wanted to help and make up for lost time. It was Lindsey that brought us back together, but our love for one another that sustains us thus far. I say Summer is like home for me because when we were teenagers, we did everything together. Everything. We even slept in the same bed. One night in October of 2022, she came and spent the night. She sat on the back porch with me with our feet kicked up and talked into the early morning hours. I took a picture of her curled up in my bed with my dogs. I was happy she was home.

I made two other friends during that time. They both came into my life unexpectedly at the right time and only stayed a short time, but they impacted my life. I won't write about them in detail but instead, leave you with poems and short stories.

Side note- thank you to my coworkers that checked in on me occasionally and never forgot about me. I can't name them all, but you know who you are. I cherish each and everyone one of you.

From left to right: Me, Leslie, Kathy, Amanda, Lindsey and Summer

Me and Dee

Me and Kat

Lindsey, Me and Les

Sister, Sister

Thank God for sisters. I was blessed with three! I keep in contact with two of them often. Audra and Lisa. Audra is five years younger than me and Lisa thirteen years younger.

We have a text thread that we chat on daily. I love the talks I have with them. Two different perspectives on life and relationships, but also we seem to have the same views ultimately.

They act as a reminder of myself a lot. Same dark humor. You know, like, don't forget who you are type of thing. I've learned I need constant reassurance, and validation, if you will, and they help provide that to me. I'm working on not needing that so much, but it takes time.

They make me laugh! I need laughter in my life. That's one thing that never fails to provide happiness and fulfillment. They offer encouraging words and that hard, honest truth at times.

I wish that everyone had a sister! They truly are the best and I'm forever grateful for the many texts shared between us.

Audra lives close by, maybe thirty minutes away, but Lisa lives on the other side of the country. I don't get to see her as often unless it's via FaceTime, but just knowing she's present in my life is precious to me.

I have another sister I haven't seen in several years and that breaks my heart, but everyone makes choices in life that we can't control. I love her from a distance. I miss her terribly, but Audra and Lisa have definitely stepped up and helped fill the void.

I hope my other sister knows how much I love and miss her. I can't wait for the day I can wrap my arms around her again. She would always give the best hugs. I'm not much of a hugger, but she would take her hugs. I'm laughing as I write this reminiscing on how my younger sister, by ten years, could tackle me to the ground just to get her hugs.

Thank you, sisters, for the love, comfort and laughs you've provided through this difficult time.

From left to right: Audra and Lisa.

From left to right: Audra and Lisa

From left to right: Lisa and Audra

This is 40

During this time, I had a birthday, of course. My 40th, to be exact. I've never been one to want a celebration, really, but it was my 40th, after all. A new beginning is how I wanted to look at it. A decade that would be different than my last. I even created a 40s bucket list of things I wanted to do before I turned 50.

There were only two people I wanted to celebrate with. Lindsey and Leslie. Those were the only two friends I had that didn't leave me when the identity theft happened. They would stop by, unannounced, of course, because they couldn't call. They'd bring me beer and sit for hours on my back porch with me. I felt protected and loved during those times. They would send me dinner. They're two very exceptional people.

Lindsey ended up not feeling well that day, but I went to Leslie's and even though she had been at work all day, she made sure to get my favorite cupcakes from a local bakery. We had pizza and cupcakes and she painted me a picture of a poppy. It sits in a frame in my room and has ever since.

The two of us, friends since teenagers, sat and laughed, cried and enjoyed a beer together on her front porch. I enjoy those moments with my dear friend.

It was enough. I was near someone I loved and someone that loved me unconditionally and I was ok with that. I appreciate you, Les!!

The day started off with a fight with my husband. He didn't wish me a happy birthday until 10:00 pm that night and it was via a Facebook post.

I started my day in tears and I ended my day in tears.

Journal Entry

January 29, 2022

Yesterday was my 40th birthday. With a pending appt @ the career center after almost a year of being sick, I can't help but wonder if it was my last. I woke up in tears because of a huge fight with ___ the night before. I am writing this @ the end of the night in tears again because of another huge fight with ___

I'm so tired. Emotionally. Physically. Spiritually, mentally. 39 was by far the hardest year to date and don't even have any answers as to why. 39 took a toll on me. A toll I don't know that I'll ever recover from.

Every year my mother sings me Happy Birthday. She always sends an email too. I heard nothing from her. I'm sure because of the identity theft.

40, I'm already tooted for you.

Acorns, Cemeteries, and Creeks

These places had become the go-to for Leslie, Lindsey and me to escape everyday problems and be able to communicate without any worry.

We would often meet at either place, mostly Lindsey and I, because Leslie worked but she always showed up when she could.

We've had many deep conversations in those places. The first time Lindsey and I went to the cemetery, it was late afternoon and the sun was starting to set. It was one of the most beautiful sunsets I'd seen. There's just something about southern Alabama in the evenings as the sun goes down. It's so peaceful.

I know you're probably thinking this is an odd place to go hang out and have a conversation, but Lindsey and I knew we'd be alone there and it would be private and it was one mile from my home.

That evening as the sun went down and it turned dark, an acorn fell and hit Lindsey. She immediately picked it up for good luck and put it in her pocket. Not long after, I had one hit me. I saved mine too. The funny thing is we both washed our jeans with the acorn still in the pocket and neither acorn was disturbed by that.

We've saved those as a reminder of our strength, just like an oak tree that can grow from something so small into something strong and mighty. It was sentimental.

The creek was the go-to for us. It's right around the corner from Lindsey's house. We'd often meet there and turn our phones off unless we wanted to capture the moment in a picture. Lindsey is the photographer. She loves to take pictures especially candid ones. I'm grateful to her for that. She captures the moments as they are. She has a gift for it.

We all had chaotic lives during this time and the ability to meet and escape for just a short while meant so much to me. We'd all sit on the pier and watch the sunset. That was usually the time of day we'd go and just for that reason. There's something about the clouds and sunlight reflecting on the water that instantly makes me feel at peace.

I still have my acorn. It sits in a jewelry box my mom made for me years ago. I will forever cherish the peaceful moments I shared with Leslie and Lindsey during this time. I was getting off the back porch. I was able to surround myself with people that loved me. I needed that more than even I knew at the time.

I truly believe that God removes people from your life that do not add and places people in your life that need to be there, if even for just a season.

When all of this happened, I hadn't been as close to either of them for a while. We all had busy lives and we just weren't able or didn't try hard enough to make time for one another. Through our situations, we found a way to be there for one another. To listen. To pour back into each other and build each other up.

Lindsey and I would spend hours on the phone, when it worked, talking and discussing creative ideas and how and what we wanted to do with our lives. At one point, we felt my life needed to be a Netflix Documentary because I literally couldn't make this up. We laughed and laughed over the idea of that.

My sister Audra would help me come up with ideas for it as well. She has excellent ideas too. That was fun for a while. I was able to escape my life and pretend for a little while even though the conversation was still about me.

Me, Leslie and Lindsey

Lindsey, Leslie and Me

Me, Leslie and Lindsey

Me

Always Wear Shoes When Walking Through BS

Always wear shoes when walking through BS. A nod to my broken toes and the BS situation I'd found myself in.

The constant conversations with Prudential for my short-term disability and my caseworker, that I could barely communicate with. The language barrier caused for many laughs and tears alike.

One day I went to my sister Audra's and as I was walking through the door, I was on the phone with my caseworker from Prudential. I had her on speakerphone because I'd been driving. I told Audra my frustrations with them and she got to hear how ridiculous it was for the first time and she could see the look of defeat and frustration on my face. The phone calls were draining. They were getting harder and harder for me to do.

She quickly grabbed the phone from me and took over the conversation. See, I'd spend 2-3 hours every day on the phone with this company. Every single day. And every day, I was told something completely different. I was so frustrated I would cuss. I would yell into the phone. I couldn't handle it anymore.

I was so grateful to her that day. She asked the names of supervisors and well, she was "the Karen" for me. The I want to speak to a manager Karen. I didn't have the fight in me anymore to do that. I only had defeat and tears. I was 102 lbs. I was fragile. My foot was broken again. And they were wanting to deny my disability because even though I had eight doctors saying I couldn't work, a nurse at Prudential makes the determination.

And they determined I could work. The thing about short-term disability that no one tells you is that once you're on it and a doctor says you can't work, you're stuck. Because when the nurse at Prudential decides you can, then the doctors have to retract their statements so you don't lose your job and you have to return against medical advice.

Bullshit huh? Thought so.

Eventually, I was approved for short-term disability and I know that Audra was one of the reasons for that. She called them out on their bullshit and they paid for six months. I continued to see the doctors as instructed and eventually, my case was sent to the long-term disability department.

What I didn't know was that the company I'd worked at for twelve years had a policy in place that terminates you once your short-term disability ends. That was for real BS.

On February 14, 2022, I was terminated for being on long-term disability through the company. They ended my employment through an eight-minute phone call. That was it. For the first time since I was fifteen years old, I was jobless. I was approved and receiving benefits from the company and yet somehow was no longer an employee. The EEOC said this is illegal. However, the statute of limitations for complaints was up. There was nothing I could do. I was devastated.

I worked so hard to do everything that was asked of me to make sure I didn't lose my job. It wasn't my fault. I was sick. I'd have several broken bones. I needed several surgeries.

After many, many phone calls and paperwork later, I got the approval for my long-term disability. I was approved for twenty-four months. Just three months into that, the nurse at Prudential made the determination that I could work and denied my disability. I no longer had an income. Unemployment has yet to pay, although I'm eligible. I've been filing for eight months now.

BS.

This is when my husband wanted to sell the house. Without my income, he didn't want to pay anything anymore or he said he couldn't afford to. Not our mortgage, not our car notes, nothing. The utilities were getting paid, barely.

Where was the money going? I couldn't log into our bank account to see. Or any account for that matter. I remember a particular day when the power bill was 900.00 and I couldn't even call the power company to find out why because the bills were in my husband's name.

Another issue I was having was with our car insurance. I'd discovered that Allstate has something they call Drivewise that you can sign up for. It's a discount program for people that allow Allstate to monitor their driving. It monitors the start and stop of your trip with GPS, the rate of speed you're driving, how many times you brake and if you're using your phone while driving. They even throw in Identity theft protection! This is my favorite part because here's yet another company that we paid (without my knowledge) to monitor our accounts.

When I was looking for the source of Wi-Fi on my car, I googled a lot. I came across Drivewise and immediately called Allstate and they confirmed we, in fact, were enrolled in the program. I was never told this. It wouldn't have served me well to have this feature because I was a shift worker and drove during the hours they consider high risk for wrecks and not to mention my lead foot.

The identity theft protection of the program would have you enter your login information for every account you want monitored so they can alert you to any changes. When Allstate confirmed I indeed had this, I asked for the login information for me to see it. I didn't have the app. Not that I could see anyway. That's weird. Yet when I went to install the app for the first time in my life, the App Store showed it had been downloaded under my Apple ID.

The Drivewise app links to your motion and fitness app that comes pre-installed on iPhones. They had to walk me through setting it up, except it'd already been set up. I had a login created for the hacked Gmail account. The motion and fitness app already had the settings on. The identity theft program had every login and password I'd ever created. So someone was getting alerts to my accounts with the updated information. They knew where I was, how fast I drove and what I was doing on my phone during that time. Something that was meant to make you safe and protect you became Stalker/Hacker 101 for someone else.

Apple explained this to me in the beginning. They told me to turn off my FaceTime feature, iMessage, uninstall the utilities such as calculator, etc., and turn off my camera and microphone in all apps because both were turning on without me even using my phone. The accessibility features were set up. There was Braille on my phone. IPhone has so many features that allow someone to track/stalk you it's ridiculous. Features they claim make things easier for you and yeah, I guess so if you don't have a stalker, but using two-factor verifications and face verification was actually making my problem worse!

I told Allstate to remove Drivewise immediately and that I needed to file a claim for identity theft. At this point, I couldn't provide a copy of the police report because it needed to be subpoenaed and it didn't really matter because, according to them, if my husband signed up for it, then the state of Alabama recognized it as "our" consent. What the? I know! I'll never forget the day they told me that. I was so angry! I wasn't allowed to remove something that tracked me? I couldn't change anything? I couldn't make a claim for identity theft? Yet the state recognized his signature as my consent, but because it's his account, I can't cancel that?! I didn't sign up for this! Literally.

Signing up for identity theft seemed to be a trend on most accounts, except no one ever let me make a claim. Here's the catch, if it's someone inside your home or someone you know, well, that's not their problem. They see it as you could be doing it to yourself and make a claim for the money. That's ridiculous, especially when it comes to AT&T who knows what's going on with your phone.

I eventually got out of my contract with AT&T with my sister Audra's help. She read through their policies and discovered that if you use their service to commit a crime in any way you get banned for life. Well, like I said, they could see everything that went on with my husband's account. I could not. Using their own policy against them, I emailed the office of the president of the company and explained I had proof of their service being used to break laws.

I'd already found the picture of my email in a crane at work. They could see the changes made to the accounts and where they originated from. My employer used AT&T and that was a huge account for them. My husband's work phone was through them. They instead chose to let me out of my contract (on my newest phone in my name) and not charge me for the phone I took a hammer to. They wiped the bill clean and wished me luck and told me not to trust anyone. Hardly a resolution.

I now needed another new phone. My sister gave me hers and she got a new one. Shortly after arriving home, the phone was hacked. I had the Bluetooth off! I didn't let it out of my sight! I hadn't signed into any accounts. What was going on? It was infuriating not to really know. Obviously, someone inside my house, I mean, I already knew the oldest daughter was assisting, but even after learning as much as I had, I was still ending up in this situation. How?!

I threw the phone in the pool the same day. I just couldn't deal with it anymore. The next day I got the pool net and scooped it out, assuming it was done for good, but Apple has another cool feature where your phone can now survive in water. Isn't that awesome? I'm laughing as I write this. It takes me back to the moments I laughed uncontrollably sometimes because of how crazy it all was. My husband would come outside and ask me what I was laughing at and I'd always answer the same, "Oh, I'm f****d!" He'd look at me like I'd lost my mind and hell, maybe I was. Who wouldn't?!

Always wear shoes...

Bossy Brisket

If there's one thing I've had the hardest time with in my life, it's someone telling me what to do. I've never taken well to that. I welcome input, opinions, etc. I, however, in the end, will do what I want.

There's a person that's in my life, although not by choice, that insists on being bossy. Insists on it. As if I would ever listen. Lmao. That will never happen. You will never get me to do what you want. Ever.

There's another person in my life, also not by choice, that allows the other person to tell them what to do. I am so disturbed by this. Why? It's not my life. It's not my problem.

I think it bothers me because I feel it's degrading to a degree. As if the person can't think for themselves. As if whatever they think or opinions they have or decisions they make aren't good enough. Wtf? Don't be with that person if you feel that way. The need to control them constantly has to be tiring.

If they say the brisket is done, trust that the damn brisket is done!

PS: You burned the damn brisket, not him.

The Desert and Changing Tides

Every now and then, you'll have someone come into your life unexpectedly. In a good way. Kind of like when you're in the dark and someone hands you a flashlight. That kind of way.

It can be relieving. Exciting. Comfortable. They just come in and that's it. You know they've impacted your life in some way. It's a changing of the tides. And they'll always leave an imprint. They've changed you.

As my sister once said, -"When your world is on fire, anyone who looks like a drop of water, you don't want to let evaporate." -Audra. So true. She has a saying called "heart holes". Kind of like filling a hole.

Here's where the desert comes in. It's dry. Its the wind. The beautiful sunsets. It's all the things. I don't want it to be just an escape. I want it to be the tide. A change for me. For the better.

I once heard a song titled The Desert and something about the lyrics in that song and the sound of the music touched my soul in a way I could never explain. It was as if it was written for that moment. For that time. That tide. I wanted to be there, in the desert.

It made me feel understood in the moment. Like someone on this earth knew what I was feeling and needed. I'm forever grateful for this.

Idk why things happen the way they do, but I've always been a strong believer that everything happens for a reason. I think no matter how long a person can stay in your life; they can impact you in such a way that you will never forget. Whether it's a friend, a lover, or an in between the two.

Thank you for that Song. Thank you for showing up when I needed it and thank you for the desert. Thank you for changing the tide and handing me the flashlight.

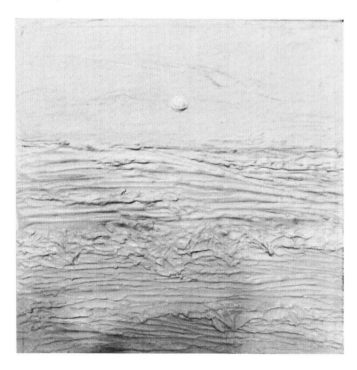

"Changing Tides"

Never give up, for that is just the place and time that the tide will turn.

-Harriet Beecher Stowe

The Tears Just Fall

In March of 2022, I'd made the decision to proceed with the divorce again. This came after my husband mentioned he wanted one twice in February.

You know how everyone has their good days and their bad? Well, this particular month, I struggled immensely. I was about to make a decision I felt based on what strangers said. Now I knew my husband had lied to me. I knew he did certain things to the accounts. I knew all of this, but for me, I felt like I was divorcing him just to fix the identity theft like the police said.

I know that sounds crazy. But that's how the trauma affected me. I was in denial. I was protecting his image. I wanted him not to be the things I'd found out. So I told myself I was divorcing him because I was told to.

I knew deep down this wasn't the case. I knew what I knew. I just didn't want to face the facts. Who does? It's hard. It's heartbreaking. It's a how can someone I love do this to me feeling.

During that month, I woke up in tears every day. I went to bed every night in tears. I couldn't understand why the tears were coming. They fell without my trying to cry. An endless stream that I could feel fall down my cheek and roll all the way down my neck. I think I cried that whole month. I'd remained strong for so long. I didn't understand why this was happening.

I've educated myself on mental health, emotional abuse and trauma. I know we can't control our feelings. I know that your mental health can affect your physical health.

My body needed to release the emotions I'd bottled up for so long. And it did. Big time. My friends would call and I could barely speak. I couldn't explain why I was crying. I was so emotional during this time. Was it because it was the beginning of the end of my marriage? My home? My life I'd built for ten years? The loss of my identity and privacy? The loss of my 401k money? My job? My health? Yes. It was all of those things.

My psychiatrist told me this would happen. She told me when the shock wears off, someone would need to be there to catch me. A therapist. I continued my therapy appointments but was too emotional to even speak. This is when I started to paint. I needed an outlet. I needed an escape. I'm so thankful I discovered something in me that I didn't have to seek help for. It was already there. I had the ability to create. Create beautiful things. I had the ability to write my feelings.

I discovered then that the only way I was going to heal was to let the emotions come, embrace them and keep going. I woke up every day with the same routine. I called it "doing the things." I'd make my bed while the coffee brewed. I unloaded and loaded the dishwasher. I vacuumed then I painted outside. I did this for a very long time. I figured if I could force myself to do the things that, I would be ok. I truly believe this helped. I didn't lay in bed. I didn't watch tv. I got up every morning around 6:00 and I did the things.

I'm truly proud of myself for this. I recorded video diaries, I wrote in my journal and I sat in silence. I shared my feelings with friends. I let the emotions come. I'm still healing. The emotions are still very much there, but I'm stronger for it.

Hardly Civil

When the police told me to get a civil attorney, I did so immediately. I spoke to five different attorneys and they all said, you guessed it. "That doesn't make any sense." They couldn't understand why the police would call this a civil matter or why they would not provide me a copy of the police report if it wasn't under investigation.

So everyone was willing to divorce me, but no one was willing or able to do anything about my situation. So I gave up. Why get a divorce if the police wouldn't help and the attorney couldn't help? I didn't know what to do. So I did nothing for seven months. It took my husband asking me to go get his belongings from the police department to light a fire under me again and fight this.

I was so upset that I wasn't even aware of him making a special trip to the police station to drop off items I didn't even know about. Why would I assume responsibility for that?

I found another attorney. This time I made sure to follow my story up with, I've already spoken to the DA and he said I could press charges, so this isn't civil. Well, this attorney decided to listen to me and actually called the DA and checked my story out. The DA confirmed what I'd said. The attorney wanted to fight for everything we could. I hired him on the spot.

I didn't tell my husband about this meeting or any other meetings I'd had with attorneys. I always parked several buildings away and would walk to their offices so he wouldn't know where I was. I kept my phone off the entire time. I was in fear for my safety because of what the police told me. So I was scared and didn't even know why or at least too traumatized to recognize the situation for what it was. Stalking, theft, wiretapping, identity theft, emotional abuse.

I said from day one, even if this was a civil matter with my husband, it was not with his ex-wife and I couldn't understand how she'd committed several felonies that I could provide proof of, and the police department would not help me. Now that made no sense! I was and am still very angry with the detectives. How can you let someone get away with what they did? How can the DA tell me one thing and the police another? It literally didn't make sense.

We did subpoena the police report and after almost a year of trying to get it, I got an email from the attorney's office on May 3, 2022. It had the police report! I couldn't believe it. There it was, the long-awaited report. It had my statement, of course, and it listed my husband and the ex-wife as suspects. Suspects in what, though? A civil matter? I was so frustrated. There it was in black and white. I knew they had the information they weren't sharing. Why were they protecting her? I knew they didn't care for my husband. But why protect her? I had proof!

He'd stopped paying our bills. Our mortgage, our car notes. I was no longer working at this point. I had to get food stamps to eat. My friends were giving me money here and there and bringing food.

This is not how I imagined my life would turn out. I was embarrassed. I didn't want handouts from anyone. I had my pride. But eventually, I accepted the situation for what it was and appreciated everyone that helped me.

Original Artwork by Brooke Howell, 2022

"Colorful Chaos"

"Sunsets are proof that no matter what happens, every day can end beautifully."-Kristen Butler

This painting was done on one of my toughest days. I wanted to prove to myself and others that something beautiful can come from the worst days.

Painting Through the Pain

My journey over the last two years has been nothing short of a Lifetime movie. This has changed my life in so many ways. I quit talking. I quit sitting inside my home. I was afraid to shower. I needed something to pass the time. Something to focus on other than the Hell I was in.

One day I decided to do something that would distract me from all of the madness and I bought a canvas. I didn't know what I wanted to paint or even how. I just wanted to paint. I thought of my friend Leslie. She loves the beach. It's her happy place. I wanted a happy place. So I painted the beach. Then I painted the beach again. And so on and so on.

My friend Lindsey said it's me painting through the pain and how right she was! That was my therapy. My escape. I hope when you look at my art, you'll see the "happy places" that I chose instead of defeat.

I've done about 100 paintings so far. Most have been gifts to friends or family. I painted Christmas ornaments in 2022 to gift. I love how they turned out. I have a few series that I've done. I pretty much just paint how I'm feeling that day. I have a sunset series titled Rayleigh. It means scattered light. It's the series I'm most proud of. I would watch the sunset every day from my back porch and study the clouds and how the sun would scatter light across the sky. Those were the most peaceful moments I've had. So that series was extremely personal to me.

I recently started sketching after a friend I made on Instagram from Belarus suggested it. We'd become fast friends and spoke daily. I decided to start with me. A self-portrait sketch, if you will. I haven't mastered faces, hands, or feet yet, but I feel it gives a signature style to the art and I love it. I've sold several paintings so far and I feel as if I've tapped into an unknown talent. Something beautiful that came from an ugly situation.

Thank you to everyone that encourages me to continue my art journey.

Rayleigh Sunset Series 2022 Brooke Howell

Journal Entry

June 3, 2022

Painting through the pain... that's what I've been doing. This last year has been so tough. I don't now how to navigate through this mess. I'm so proud of myself for being able to survive so far. Still no resolve. Still no answers. Little hope. How does one recover from this? Rebuild? Start over? Escape? Make it stop? Sit and Paint.

B

Don't Play A Victim, Don't Be A Victim

Don't play a victim. Don't be a victim. This is something that my therapist told me. She said I had learned helplessness. I wasn't exactly sure what that meant at the time, but she described me as being like a dog inside of a fence that had an opening, but I refused to go out. That I would rather stay inside the fence than attempt to go out of the opening. She also told me that if I act like a victim, I will be treated as such. So, by me tiptoeing around, by me trying to make myself smaller, by me constantly apologizing for things that I haven't done wrong, that I'm playing a victim, and so I'm being treated as such by the person that's treating me that way.

I heard what she said and I thought to myself, okay, so basically, stand up for myself, but no need to yell and shout because I'm not a confrontational person. And well, obviously, I made myself as small as can be because I don't want any type of confrontation, which is why I apologize all the time. I tested this theory out one day. I wanted to talk about that because I actually did become a victim because I stood up for myself. I can't help but wonder if I became a victim because I was trying not to play the victim.

One night I got home after being at Lindsey's house; I entered through the front door as always; I walked through the house, through the laundry room that was connected to our garage, where my husband spent all of his time. Opened the garage door and said, "Hey, I just wanted to let you know that I'm home."

He immediately says to me that I needed to quit talking about his ex-wife and the fact that she's pregnant. Well, I just recently found out she was pregnant that day by him. I didn't know that this was a big secret. I mean, we are in our forties. I didn't know we were hiding pregnancies this late in our life. I told everybody that would listen, just because I thought it was odd. Why is she trying to hide her pregnancy? The person that wants to come and get into my mailbox, the person that had stolen my information, I don't understand why I need, I, me specifically, needs to not run my mouth about her and not talk about the fact that she's pregnant. Well, keep in mind at this point, she was like seven months pregnant. I didn't know that. I just knew she was pregnant. I thought early stages, but either way, it did not matter. She was pregnant and apparently trying to hide it, I guess.

I stuck my hand in the air and pointed toward my husband, and I said, "Do not ever tell me who I can and cannot talk about. Do not ever tell me what

I can and cannot say. I will do whatever I want to do because I'm grown."

Well, before I knew it, my husband bolted across the garage running full force at me. He had a drill in his hand, a cordless drill; I guess whatever he was working on, he was already holding it. I'm not sure. Everything kind of became blurry at that moment because it happened so quickly. My husband had never been physical with me. My husband and I, well, we never really fought. So this caught me off guard. As he's running full force towards me, I'm just standing in the doorway of the laundry room and the garage, and I don't flinch.

I don't move. I don't do anything. And the next thing I knew, he slammed me into the metal door to the garage, and I walked away. I walked into the kitchen and I started making myself a cup of coffee. It's 10:30 at night on a Saturday night, and I'm making coffee in the kitchen and I'm shaken up. I don't understand what just happened. I didn't try to defend myself in any way. I didn't move. Like I said, I didn't flinch; I didn't do anything. And that's all he did until he walked into the kitchen, and I'm not even exactly sure what he was saying to me anymore at that point, but he slung a stack of paper plates at me, not the cheap little flimsy kind. We had heavy-duty, almost like cardboard paper plates, because, lets face it, I was done washing dishes for anybody at that point.

He slung the entire stack at me and it hit me in my back, and I didn't turn around. I just said, "Well, is it yours?" Talking about the baby, because what would spark such a reaction? Why are we defending her? He knew what she had done to me. Why is he standing up for her and this baby? She's married; whose is the baby? Kind of thing. Well, when I did that, he raised his fist in the air at me. He wanted to punch me. So don't play a victim. Don't be a victim mentality here. I stuck my finger up one more time and I said to him, "Do not ever put your hands on me again."

He walked off. I grabbed my phone. I text a friend and let her know that my husband had put his hands on me. She immediately said, "I'm in the car. I'm on the way." I instructed her not to come because if there's another thing that I had learned in therapy, it was a physical abuser will usually harm family or friends just to get to you. Now, I don't know if this is true; this is just what I've been told. I told her, do not come. She told me to call the police. Well, I'm not calling the police, the same police that wouldn't help me, the same police that interrogated me, the same police that accused me of trying to adopt the children. No, I'm not calling them. I would be bleeding out in the street and someone else would have to call before that phone call would get made. I can guarantee you that.

Well, I went to the bathroom and I started taking pictures because I discovered that I had red marks all over my arms. I discovered that my elbow had been injured. It was swollen, it was bruised, and then my lip was swollen and red. I had been hit in the face, but I don't recall getting hit in the face. I guess when you're in a scuffle, you don't really know what all is going on. At least, that was the first time for me. But, apparently, something happened.

I made a decision that night. I would not call the police. However, I would go to the doctor first thing that Monday morning. I had my mother call the doctor's office and ask them if they had a responsibility or liability for reporting domestic violence if someone came in and said that they had been in an altercation or had been abused by their domestic partner. They said yes. Lindsey went with me to the doctor's office. I drove to her home because my car had wifi on it. I didn't want my husband to know where I was going. I drove to her home and we took her vehicle to the doctor's office. We go in, and I'm being seen for my elbow, which is still swollen and it hurts.

And they asked me, "Well, what happened? Did you fall?" And I said, "No. My husband slammed me into a metal door."

And the look on the nurse's face was kind of shock; I guess because I said it so matter-of-factly, so directly and without change in my voice or emotion at all, which is what I'm apparently being known for, I can tell some really hard things and not show emotion. She then apologized to me and I was like, yeah, it's fine. The doctor comes in and he asks me the same thing. So tell me what happened. I said, "Oh, well, my husband slammed me into a door." "Hmm, okay.", he said. They're making notes. They documented all of this and I thought, okay, so they're going to call the police because I damn sure wouldn't. Well, come to find out, I'd injured my synovial sac on my elbow and I had to be put in a sling, and if it wasn't going to heal properly in so many days, then I could possibly need surgery on it. After a steroid shot and an arm sling and an ace bandage later, I left and went back with Lindsey to get my car.

I was already planning to leave to go visit my mother in two days. On Wednesday, I was supposed to fly out to Mom's. I decided that I would just go home and get my suitcases, pack them up, throw some clothes in there and leave. And that's exactly what I did. Well, of course, my husband monitored everything. So we had our ring doorbell camera that caught me rolling my suitcases out the front door and into my car and I left. Well, he knew this was early. He knew when I was supposed to leave, and he was planning on taking me to the airport.

I went and stayed at Lindsey's house and I did not answer any of his phone calls for two weeks. I flew out as planned. I filed for divorce and I had him served by a private process server during that time. He was enraged; he was confused. He didn't understand because how could I, the person that is there no matter what would never leave, would never stand up for herself, would never do anything, could do this to him in such a dirty way. He had no idea that this was coming. Although in February of 2022, he asked me for a divorce and told me he wanted a divorce, but two months later, in April, he was shocked by it, shocked. I refused to speak to him until he calmed down. Finally, he did. We had the conversation. I explained why I'm doing what I'm doing. He knew that the police already told me that I needed to get a divorce in order for them to help me further.

I knew that the police had told me that, eventually, he will get physical, and he did. I was afraid to go home, but I wanted to go home. I spoke with my therapist several times while I was out of state. I spoke with my mother every day, my father every day, my brother, and my friends, trying to figure out why did I feel the need to want to go home so badly? I wanted to just go home. So against everyone, and I mean everyone's advice, I went home and when I got home, my husband had written me a very long letter, and to be honest with you, unless I went and got the letter out and read it to you, I can't tell you what it says. I'm not much of a reader anyway. I'm a scanner. I scan paragraphs and page after page, just looking for keywords that'll stand out to me.

I'm guessing there wasn't really anything that stood out to me because I can't recall what the letter said, and that was one of four that he had written me. They were very lengthy letters.

The point is that my husband decided he did not want a divorce. He had not done anything wrong. He had not done this to me. He was not a wife-beater. He was none of the things that he was being accused of, and he didn't understand my behavior. He was very distraught and upset over this. I'm not really sure why. You know, part of me thought, oh, well, he does love me, but actions speak louder than words. I know you hear that all the time. I heard it all the time. But it is so true. Actions really do speak louder than words, especially when you can't hear any more words and you can't read any more words.

You sit back, be quiet, pay attention, watch their actions, and I can promise you, they don't match.

I did that for a year and a half. I sat in silence and I watched and I paid attention. Did I solve everything? No. Was I able to prove that it was all him? No. Do I have proof of the ex-wife and the child? Absolutely. Did I find inconsistencies in his story? Yes. Did I find proof of things throughout the house that would indicate that the police might be right? Yes. But I never once told him what I knew or what I had found out. I never asked him about anything, ever. Not one time.

I did share with him in February 2022 that when I turned my contacts on in iCloud, I would see his contacts. Apple told me not to program anyone on my phone. The contacts were people he worked with and he couldn't explain that. So even when I tried, I was always given the same reasons. "I don't know" or "That doesn't make any sense."

I guess he genuinely was confused and shocked because, see, I wouldn't talk on the phone. I wouldn't talk out loud at all because if it didn't come out of my mouth, then no one could hear it. No one could record it. So the conversations that I did have with friends were had at the creeks or the cemeteries where we would leave our phones turned off in our vehicles, and we'd walk as far away from the vehicle as we could and we'd have private conversations. That's how I got my information out. For a year and a half, I lived that way.

It doesn't seem like during that timeframe that it felt hard to do, but now that I'm no longer in that situation, I can't imagine having to do that again. I can't imagine having to be quiet to control my feelings to such a degree. The only explanation I can come up with is that I was in shock throughout the entirety of my situation. That, or I'm just a very remarkable person, but I have a feeling that I was just in shock, honestly. So don't play a victim. Don't be a victim. Good luck with that.

Calm Before the Storm

There's something about the stillness that surrounds you before the storm hits. The feeling in the air... you know the storm is coming, but it's peaceful. It's quiet. You're still ok.

You know things are about to get worse and you anticipate that. You're not unaware, but the calm before the storm is just that. It's the feeling of peace before the unpeacefulness (yes, I made that word up).

I know it'll get worse before it gets better. I know. I'm enjoying the peace of still being able to paint while the storm is coming.

Original Artwork by Brooke Howell

Smunchies, Weed, and Vacation

In April of 2022, I decided to get off the back porch and go see my mom and my brother. I have severe anxiety and the fact that I was even able to do this is still shocking to me. I haven't flown on a plane alone since I was 16. It had been a minute.

The morning I was to board the plane, it was hectic. I had a full-blown anxiety attack. Lindsey's husband had to help get my suitcase closed. Lindsey and I both tried to sit on it. The night before, my friend Dee brought me a bag of winter clothes, it was still cold where I was going even though it was April, and the morning I left, Dee brought me two beers to drink to calm my nerves, a sweet note of encouragement and some wired headphones. This was the best gift. The headphones. She knew I was afraid to use Bluetooth anything at that point and she wanted me to be able to listen to music on the plane. After being escorted to the airport by Lindsey and her mom and dad. I got on the plane. It really does take a village sometimes.

Let me just first say, if you've never flown first class. Do it. It's just better in all the ways.

Once I arrived at my destination. I waited on my mom and brother to show up. They looked sad. I wasn't the same Brooke they'd seen last time. I was fragile and broken. They both teared up. I knew the toll that this situation had taken on me was visible.

I can't tell you how at peace I was when I was there. She lives in the northeastern part of the US and it's beautiful there. Very different scenery than Alabama.

I'm not sure if it was the cooler weather, but my legs started clearing up. I was able to eat. Maybe just removing myself from a stressful situation? Idk. My mom cooked all of my favorite meals, tucked me in at night and let me nap as much as I needed to.

I continued to keep my trauma therapy appointments while there and stayed in touch with my close friends and family that never left my side.

We visited Priest Lake while there and it was absolutely beautiful. I felt so good! I didn't feel sick, stressed, or worried about anything.

I do not ever smoke weed, but this day I decided to buy some. It's legal where we were. I asked for something that wouldn't make my heart pound. The guy behind the counter winked and said, "Girl

Scout cookie." Girl Scout Cookie it was! I was so relaxed and in a very creative mood.

Lindsey happened to call while I was in that "mood," and she asked if I've ever had Munchies. I was laughing so hard that I almost snorted. All I heard was munchies (of course, I had them) and she was talking about the snack. I'd never heard of the snack Munchies. I immediately messaged Frito Lay and gave them a recipe for a salty and sweet version! I named it Smunchies. I had a great day that day.

After gaining eight pounds and my skin clearing up, it was time to go back home. I was quickly reminded of everything I'd forgotten while gone. While in the DFW airport, my left leg just quit working. I went to take a step and my leg didn't come with me. I fell and I fell hard. It echoed. I cried. I cried out of anger. I was angry at my body. I was returning home. Why? What was I doing to myself, I thought.

I cried on the plane home. I cried when I went to bed that night. I didn't understand why I wanted to return to a place that was making me worse. It's really hard to explain unless you've experienced trauma, but there's a bond that forms and a connection to the place where it happened. In some weird way, I was comfortable. I was home.

I started losing weight rapidly soon after arriving home. It was hard to eat again. The nodules on my legs returned. The one thing all of the doctors agreed on was that stress would make whatever was wrong with my body worse, like gas to a fire. This trip was proof to me that they were right.

Me

Me and Mom

Me and mom's dog Harley

Me

I Apologize

Sorry, Not Sorry

I'm sorry. It's something I say. A lot. My therapist says it's "learned behavior." I apologize for things that aren't my fault. I apologize for being too loud or too anything. I try to make myself smaller so others don't feel intimidated. I'm sorry for being sorry. It's like I walk on eggshells all the time.

Weird right? I know. Sorry. Haha Still working on that. When I visited my mom in April of 2022, she said, "Quit apologizing! What happened to my daughter? You tip-toe around and whisper!" She didn't recognize me anymore. I'd become this shell of a person. I've always had this huge personality and here I was saying I'm sorry because I tiptoed a little too loud that morning and she woke up.

I didn't know I was doing it until she pointed it out. Then I would catch myself. It was hard to unlearn that. It was hard to remember who I used to be and to be able to say what was on my mind, no matter how inappropriate or embarrassing. To laugh until I snort. I had to learn those things all over again. I'm still learning.

I'm learning that it doesn't matter what other people think or what they believe. What matters is me. I hadn't put myself first since I started my relationship with my husband. It'd been ten years of me slowly turning into who I'd become. The frog. The frog in the pot of boiling water.

Getting Spiritual

I've always prayed. I may not do it the right way and no one's seen me in a church in twenty years at least. But I've always prayed. I've always believed in God.

During the most difficult times in my life, I'd pray for myself. All the other times just a routine "watch over my family and friends." But this time, after many talks with my mom, I learned how to pray for me every day and to be thankful every day for what I still had.

My prayers typically started and ended with God protecting me mentally, physically, spiritually and emotionally. I would pray for him to send angels to surround me throughout the day and stand me back up when I was falling. I lean on him a lot these days. It's something I should've been doing my whole life.

Every night I thank God that I still had a roof over my head, a car in the driveway, and food in my stomach. I knew that although things weren't good by any means, they could always be worse.

I found myself encouraging my friends to pray and pray for themselves and, to be specific. I've prayed with them.

Thank you, God, for always watching over me and providing for me.

Desperate Prayer

I've suffered a lifetime's worth of suffering. I've cried a lifetime's worth of tears. My dues have been paid, plus interest. I am tired. I am defeated. I'm done. Please, God, let that be enough already. I can't handle anymore. I've carried great weight in my life. I've carried others as well. I've been a good person. I've done good things. I have always had good intentions. I've never been malicious. I've never wished anyone harm. I've always just been a pure heart. I've loved so deeply that it's taken everything from me. I've given what hasn't been taken. There's nothing left, God. Nothing. I'm so tired. Please let this be enough. Please. I'm so empty I'm numb. I don't know what to do. I don't know how to recover anymore God. Please help me. I can't do this anymore. I'm so tired. Please hear me.

Journal Entry

July 22, 2022

Thankful for confirmations and friends.

♡B

Blooming Onions 2022, original artwork by Brooke Howell

Why some onions bloom and some don't...

It's all in the timing: when you planted your onion crop and what the weather was like can all play tricks on an onion's natural life cycle.

When an onion plant prematurely sends out a flower stalk, it's referred to as onion bolting. Onion bolting is a natural process that occurs when the plant is under stress.

You Can't Tell Me How I'm Feeling

Feelings Or Facts

You can't tell someone how they're feeling. Well, because it's their feelings. I've always had a habit of addressing tough situations or starting conversations with "I feel like..." or "You made me feel." I think it's important. It doesn't matter if you're right or wrong with feelings. What matters is how it made you feel.

I feel like I'm right about a lot of things. I feel like I'm wrong about a few. I feel as if people thought I was crazy and didn't believe me.

See? Impactful. Not wrong or right because they're feelings. I can tell you the day I left the police station... I felt like I didn't know my place anymore. I felt lost. I felt helpless. I felt scared. I felt alone. Should I have felt those things? I still don't know. They didn't give me any facts.

I feel as if I'll never know what happened to me. I feel as if the two people I know for a "fact" who had something to do with this will never get punished. I feel like that is what is making me "crazy."

I feel like I'm not getting justice. I feel angry, sad, defeated and alone. And those are facts. My feelings are my facts.

I led with my feelings in my decision-making throughout this healing journey. I knew the facts but was in denial for the most part. I felt as if I had to get a divorce. I had to remove myself. I guess some would call this intuition. I just call it my feelings.

"Journey"

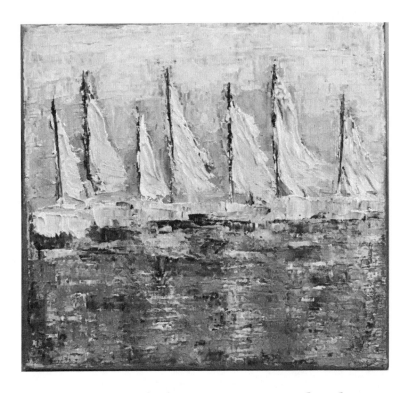

Sailboats symbolize journey and adventure. They also are associated with being carried along by the "breath of life," as its primary form of momentum is gained through the wind in its sails.

"To get through the hardest journey we need take only one step at a time, but we must keep on stepping."

-Chinese Proverbs

"Life is a journey. How we travel is up to us. We can just flow with the tide or follow our own dreams."

-Paulo Coelho

"It is the set of the sails, not the direction of the wind that determines which way we will go."

-Jim Rohn

All Mirror, No Smoke

Ever meet a person and think, bullshit, after everything they say? Yeah, same.

I recently met someone that, for whatever reason, I haven't had that bullshit feeling yet. It's unknown territory for me. It's like I'm waiting for the smoke.

I don't believe things people say anymore unless they're my friends. That's it.

Maybe that's why. Maybe this person has become my friend so I believe them. Idk. Still working on that one.

Ever owned a floor-length mirror? If not, you should. Why? Because you can see your whole self in them. No bullshit. You can see everything. I love that. Nothing is hidden.

When I meet someone, I want to see everything. No smoke, no bullshit. Just their true self. The whole thing. Like a floor-length mirror. No matter who they are to me. I ask a ton of questions. I'm a curious person.

Point is, I'm thankful I'm feeling like there's no smoke yet. It's refreshing.

All Smoke, No Mirror

Isn't it funny how you can jinx yourself by saying something you think is a good thing, but quickly you realize just by saying it, you've somehow jinxed yourself?

That's what happened to me. I wrote a thing. I meant the thing. I sent the thing. Next thing I know, smoke!

Why? Idk. Did I jinx myself? Idk. Was he just a jerk? Could be. I'll never know. Because he didn't give me a chance to. One week. That's all I needed.

I've never in my whole experienced rejection. This is hard. It's hurtful. It's confusing. It's new territory. I feel like I did something wrong. I feel like I need a chance to fix it.

It's the not knowing that's hard for me. How can I change something if I don't know? And then again, why would I want to change anything?! I'm me. I'm a lot. I'm a little. I'm in between. For whoever I want to be those things for. So it is what it is and I am who I am. That should be good enough.

So if knowing that, why do I feel upset? Idk. Because it's mean? Hurtful? Sure.

Stop blowing smoke, people. Be real. Be raw. Be you, unapologetically you. Be the mirror.

Investments

I gave you my time
It was my choice
I could've said no
But couldn't find my voice

It was easy for me
I didn't have to question
I just wish I could've seen
You weren't where I should've invested

Investing is a gift
It shouldn't be taken lightly
To give someone's time
And not return it slightly
The most precious thing

I had to offer
Was myself
And you didn't care
I told you things about me
I cannot repair

I told You to be a man

Don't ghost me

Tell me where I stand

I'm better than that

I'm grown

I've made mistakes

I own

You were an investment

It wasn't my best

I can't get back what I gave

Now I'm learning to save

Encouraging Words

(Text From Audra)

But… whether you tell him you have feelings too, and have every right to those as well, is up to you, of course. And maybe being this vulnerable is where you're at in *your* place. And maybe meeting people where they're at in their lives isn't a bad thing.

And as for your video diary… I hope you can know and understand that missing ****, or just his company, would be completely normal even in a "regular divorce." You are experiencing one of the most intense trauma bonds there are: narcissistic abuse is incredibly damaging. You're feeling all the things. You're fragile. You're trying to heal but you're hurting. And you know what? Sometimes hurting people *can* be mean. Because any extra boo-boos on top of the wounds that are already there is fkn painful. People in pain lash out. They cry. They feel anger. They might even be looked at as "immature."

Those are all perfectly normal responses to a totally abnormal, adverse experience.

So like I said... people meeting you where you're at... is important. They need to be able. If they're not - those are not your people anymore. Your people will change because you change. It's not always bad. But change isn't always comfortable, either. And neither are shitty mattresses. I wish I had one or a better one or something but I didn't get that far rip.

I just want you to know... like KNOW... that you are not disappointing anyone by taking care of yourself as best you can. And that's your priority right now. So... tell those ideas to stfu because they just don't know any different yet. YET.

And you're loved. So much. There's that too.

Lol. Well. Ps... sometimes our pain needs (and deserves) a voice too. It's not a bad thing to let it be heard - even when it's not so pleasant to hear.

-Audra

From left to right: Audra and I

Who Would've Thought? Not Me

Problem-Solving 101

Analytical. That's me. That's my brain. I'm a problem solver. I have the ability to look at a situation and find a solution.

Yet somehow, I've found myself in an unworkable situation. How's that? There's always a loophole. There's always a way around.

Is it because I'm emotional? Idk. For the first time in my life, I cannot solve a problem. I don't have the ability to do it.

I'm feeling defeated and tired. I feel like I'm missing the key thing I need to make it work. What is it?! I give up already! Someone tell me what to do. I literally don't know. Me. The analytical thinker. The person that was paid to think... analytically. It's laughable, really. How does someone do that for a living but can't solve what should be an easy problem to solve?

Emotions. Or corrupt companies and institutions? I mean, let's face the facts here. I have solid proof. Undeniable proof of what happened to me and who did it. Did you know that most people that experience identity theft never know who did it? That's right. And I did. And no one cares. Not any of the companies that I did business with. Not my job, not the police and apparently now, not the district attorney's office.

Could you imagine having all the evidence needed to put someone in jail for life possibly if you add all the felonies together, and every one turns their head like they didn't see or hear it? That's what happened. Is happening. It's messed up. It's not justice. I couldn't even get a protective order against the person that I could prove was stalking me.

I'm in this alone and I want everyone to know it so they can be prepared to also not receive help. Not here. Not in Alabama. Apple always said I would never recover from this; that's how bad it was. I choose not to believe that. I will recover from this because I'm a fighter and I'll be damned if I let some entitled ex-wife think she's going to get away with what she did. Child neglect? Idk. I would hope that charges be brought in the fact that she used her child to commit felonies. But what do I know? Maybe it's just my analytical thinking I'm doing. Just trying to find a way.

My goal is to eventually get a bill passed to help protect people from stalking. Especially married individuals in the state of Alabama where a car insurance company claims one signature represents you both. To help obtain information from your employer regarding your own paystub instead of conflating married couples because they work for the same company.

I will do whatever I can to help others in similar situations. I may not have been able to change my situation, but I will do what I can to help change others. I will speak out on it.

The Garage

My husband started spending hours and hours inside the garage. What was he doing in there? I wasn't exactly sure. I'd gotten used to it.

I don't know how long it'd been going on because I'd worked shift work. I was exhausted most of the time, but the minute I switched positions in the company and was on day shift, I was home when I normally wasn't and I started noticing things that maybe I was too tired to notice before or maybe didn't even happen while I was there.

I interrupted something when I got my new work schedule. I think the garage was something that'd been going on for longer than I knew.

I called it tinkering. My husband would spend hours rewiring lights and "fixing" things that weren't broken. Like our vacuum. This had become obsessive behavior.

I didn't understand it at the time. I just thought he was stressed because of work. That seemed to be his go-to answer, but he was isolating himself from me.

As the days went on, the hours spent in the garage got longer. I started making notes of everything he was working on in the house. Why wouldn't I? It was different. It was weird.

He changed our door locks four times to add keypads, the doorbell three, and the smart light bulbs in our home at least twice. He installed dimmer switches, changed our Wi-Fi router three times, put up numerous solar lights in the backyard and then would work on them and clean them constantly. As you can imagine, for someone who's been traumatized by electronics and now my husband is fascinated with them, I was disturbed. I was upset. I felt it was on purpose. It caused me unnecessary paranoia.

I couldn't help but ask what he was doing. He would get so frustrated when I'd ask why we needed a new lock on the door or why he was changing the doorbell out again.

It got so bad that I just didn't even ask anymore. I just let it be. My husband started sleeping on our sofa because he'd spend so many hours in the garage and he'd say he didn't want to wake me when he came to bed. He slept on the sofa for a year at least.

I'm sure some of you know someone with this type of behavior. You may recognize it. You may know what I'm talking about. It took me a little while to figure it out.

Money Doesn't Talk

Income A Must

Anyone remember the days when if you had cash, you had leverage? You could negotiate. You could get anything. Not anymore. Who knew?

I found out today that no matter how much cash you have, without a job or good credit, you can't even rent a place to live.

18,000 cash. That's how much I offered for a place today.

So now what? What does one do when one can't even get a decent hotel room unless you have a credit card? Not a damn thing. That's what. Not. A. Damn. Thing.

This world is so messed up. Seriously though. Messed all the way up. I've been living like it's the 90s because of my situation. Cash only. No choice.

I've sold my home. I have money and I can't do a damn thing with it. I swear, sometimes I wonder how I've survived this nightmare. I wonder how the ex-wife has survived doing this for so long.

You don't do this to someone. Get up off your behind and work for your own things! Don't take someone else's. Don't think anyone owes you anything because they don't!

I can only hope that one day you'll find yourself helpless as you've made me..

In the end, with a really good friend to co-sign, I was able to rent with a full year paid upfront.

Bear and Gilly

A Girl's Best Friend

Dogs. Man's best friend. They say that for a reason. They're loyal. They love unconditionally.

In October of 2016, my husband brought home two boxer puppies. Sweet right? Well, that day, I was in tears. See, we'd already lost two boxers to cancer. We were still grieving. We decided to get another one. ONE. I expressed how important it was for me to be able to let the dog pick me.

The dog was for me, after all. The two before were actually his before we married. After weeks of looking, I had an appointment to go see a specific one. While out shopping with my sister, one day, my husband calls and asked me to come home. He had a surprise for me.

As I walked in, he placed two boxer puppies in my arms. He'd gone and picked out not one but two puppies. One white (Bear) and one brown (Gilly).

Now some people may think, aww, that's so sweet. I didn't feel that way. It felt controlling. Like once again, he took away something from me. As I sat there holding these puppies, I cried and cried.

217

I'm a huge dog lover. And after all, these were sweet little puppies who didn't ask to be taken from their mom. Of course, I love them. I took care of them from that point on.

I fed them. I bathed them. I spent time with them. Bear took to me immediately. Gilly was always standoffish. She took more to him. Well, at least for the first five years.

One day, not long after, finding out I was sick. Gilly started following me everywhere I went. She wouldn't stop. She wouldn't leave my side. If I stayed outside in 30-degree weather, so did she. It didn't matter to her. She hasn't left my side in almost two years now. Not for a second.

He wants my dogs. My dogs. The dogs that were a gift. The ones that only I take care of. The ones that never leave MY side. How could something that was supposed to be sweet end so sad? It's as if I knew the day I held them, I was going to lose them.

I have conversations with Gilly often and I let her know that I love her so so much. That I will always love her. She listens so intently. She will stare into my eyes as I explain, "Momma has to go bye-bye, but she will always love you."

She knows. She's sad. She knows what that means. She has double hip dysplasia and she's in pain quite often. She needs her mom. And I won't get to be there for her anymore.

I've lost everything. And now I'm losing my best friends, that have literally remained by my side day in and day out. My feelings aren't considered but consider theirs. They'll grieve me. Gilly will decline. I know it. He wrote in the divorce papers that he would not inform me of anything going on with them. I will never get to see them again.

What an asshole. My heart is in pieces.

UPDATE- 11/3/2022 I was able to bring my sweet puppies with me. My ex-husband decided not to keep them after all. After a large pet deposit and vet bills later, they were home. I boarded them for two days until we both were moved and settled. I was so excited. I wouldn't be alone and I'd have my dogs that stayed by my side throughout this process.

It wasn't long before the threats of taking them from me started. Well, not them, Bear. He only wanted Bear. I wouldn't give him up. I've fought hard, he was a gift to me, but somehow my ex-husband feels as if he can take Bear. That's his dog, according to him. Well, honestly, I've thought about it. They do miss him. But won't they miss each other more? They're siblings, after all. They're sitting right by my side as I write this. Loyal until the end.

Gilly and Bear

Bear

Gilly

It's Final

Was It Worth It?

On December 2, 2023, my divorce was final. I found out through an email I'd received from the secretary of my attorney. I can't really describe how I felt. It felt unreal. Like it didn't really happen. It was as if the last ten years of my life didn't even deserve a phone call to let me know. It felt like I was reading about the passing of a loved one. It felt so permanent. I knew my now ex-husband probably didn't know yet because he didn't use an attorney.

I debated on telling him. I can't recall if I ever did. He was upset with me for us moving and me divorcing him. It's like he'd forgotten that he's asked me for a divorce twice. Like he'd forgotten that he said he couldn't live this way anymore.

He told me before the divorce I was letting her win (the ex). I didn't care what anyone thought. I needed to remove myself from any connection with her, him, and the children. It had to be done. I felt I didn't have a choice. And well, let's face it, the police and the district attorney's office refused to help unless I did, so what else was I going to do? Every marriage has its problems, but without having full knowledge of what happened or the extent of his involvement, how would I ever know if the issues we had could've been worked out?

That day I went out shopping and out to lunch with Leslie and Lindsey. We all had some last-minute Christmas shopping to do and honestly, I needed the distraction. I didn't know what I was feeling. Relief? Sadness? Defeat? Maybe I felt them all. But we had a nice lunch at a local pub where you can hang a dollar bill up with your name. I decided to write "Cheers to a new life." I felt it was the beginning of the end of a very painful journey. I had hope for the future.

I had an upcoming appointment with the gastroenterologist scheduled for January to go over my latest abdominal ultrasound and EGD results. I wasn't looking forward to this appointment because we'd also be discussing sending me to the Mayo Clinic. I didn't want to go. Shortly after being notified of the divorce, it occurred to me that I couldn't go even if I wanted to because I no longer had health insurance.

I'd been on my husband's insurance since we were married. Now, what would I do? I was semi-relieved to know I didn't have to go to the doctor, but also panicked because I could no longer afford my medication either. What was I going to do now?

I found myself feeling helpless all over again, but for different reasons now.

It wasn't long after that I contacted the district attorney's office as instructed. I was ready to press the charges he said I could. I've emailed, left voicemails and made numerous phone calls. I've yet to hear back from anyone. I sit on my back porch, yes, I still do that, as I write this on January 26, 2023.

I started emailing the detectives again. After many, I did receive one short email from one of the detectives stating that because this was a civil matter, they'd closed the case! What?! What is she talking about? The district attorney's office said criminal. They filmed me and interrogated u. They made me subpoena the police report. They listed me as a victim on the report. Civil?! I'm so sick of hearing that!

This is not civil! Stalking, stealing, HIPPA violations, honestly, what is civil about that and when did the ex become part of this being civil? She should've already been sentenced, in my opinion.

I was told by the detective that if I'm still experiencing problems, I'd need to make a new report in the city in which I currently live. I couldn't believe it. The district attorney's office said criminal and to press charges. So what are they talking about?! Separate myself from my husband and they'd help me. What changed and when was anyone going to tell me?! I felt all over again like I didn't know why I even got a divorce. For what?! To be in just another messed up situation alone? It's in these times I forget the why.

I have a lot of anger. Of course, this is still going on. My credit is ruined. My 401k money is gone. I got the divorce I was told to get. I've lost my home, my family, my privacy, my health and my job. Of course, I was still dealing with this. No one has helped me. No one has told me how to recover from this.

I recently went out to eat and a show with three couples and myself. I missed him more than ever that night. Why? Because he was my person? Or because, for the first time in a long time, the chair next to me was empty? Because the passenger seat was empty? Because I had to drive alone, check into a hotel alone? I don't know.

I've chosen to embrace whatever feelings I have and be ok with that. They are my feelings and however right or wrong they may be, I still feel them. I'm not angry at myself for that. I was a victim. I didn't do anything wrong. So for me, it's ok to miss him. I'm sure once the shock wears off, it'll hit me like a ton of bricks and I'll grieve our marriage. Right now, I'm still trauma bonded. I am not ashamed of that.

We want to protect them. Rationalize and explain things away. I did that. I blamed the whole situation on his ex-wife and their oldest child. I knew he had lied to me, but the bond was there. I was protecting his reputation. I didn't want people to know that side of him.

I'm slowly starting to separate my feelings from facts. It's a very slow process for me, but through therapy, I've been able to see the difference and I'm starting to accept that it's perfectly normal to have the feelings I have but also to understand the reality of it.

Facts: I found emails he kept from me. He had access to my accounts that he knew I was trying to regain access to. He had DriveWise on our car insurance that tracked everything I did, including where I was and how fast I drove and monitored every account and password change. He did that.

Feelings: He loved me. He denies any wrongdoing. He swears he could never lie to me or do this. I believed him even knowing the facts.

As I sit here writing today, all of the emotions come flooding back. I feel as if I'll never get a resolution. My ex-husband sits across from me as I write this. He stops by at least once a week. He helps with things around the house and visits with the dogs.

We have an odd relationship. The bond between us will never go away; I don't think. We are able to sit comfortably in each other's presence. It's weird, I know. It's the trauma bond. It's what I'm still working on. I don't expect anyone to understand my feelings because I don't understand them myself.

I often hug him bye. He stands there and just lets me hug him for as long as I need to. This was something he'd always done. I appreciated him for that. He always knew when I needed a hug. If I didn't come to him, he would tell to come here and he'd pull me in and hug me as tight as he could. It always made me feel better.

These are the moments I miss. It's as if the last two years didn't happen. Now that I'm not living in the situation I sometimes forget how I felt. I miss him. I miss the comfort of him. He had a way of being able to calm me down. Of course, he understood me like no one else. He'd lived with me for almost ten years.

The anger I feel is sometimes so great that I can't even speak. I can't find the words to describe it. I'm angry that this happened and I don't know everything there is to know. I'm angry that I was happy until I noticed unicorns on my phone. I'm angry that I noticed anything at all because ignorance is bliss, right?

Learned Helplessness

Well, I did it. I got the divorce. I sold the house. I got the dogs. So why do I feel worse? That's weird, right? I left this crippling situation and yet I miss it. Stockholm syndrome much? Maybe. It's a thing.

As I sit here on my back porch, I find myself feeling more alone than I ever have in my life. I have friends. I have family. So why do I feel this way? Idk.

Learned helplessness-Learned helplessness is a state that occurs after a person has experienced a stressful situation repeatedly. They come to believe that they are unable to control or change the situation, so they do not try — even when opportunities for change become available.

Years. I considered it loyalty. It's not. See, it's a behavior I learned. I stay because I don't see how I can't. Literally.

I want to go back because it's where I feel "safe," "and comfortable."

A trauma bond was created. A bond that no one other than the person that did this could have with you. You're forever connected in this way. It's the person that "gets" you and "understands" your odd behavior. It's messed up!

Music To My Ears

In December of 2022, I made the decision to finally get the screen fixed in my car. This was a huge deal, but I'd removed myself from the situation and I felt it was time. I knew that I couldn't continue living without technology.

When I broke the screen with the hammer two years prior, it took away my ability to have a backup camera, navigation and radio. A friend I made along the way recommended someone he knew to fix it for me. He suggested Wayne. Wayne happened to be someone I've known for a very long time.

I immediately reached out to him and he agreed to fix it for me. I ordered the part and in one day, it was done.

And to hear the music... Like, "What?" I didn't realize how I'd lived for almost two years and it felt good. Music is so healing for the soul and to be able to turn the radio up as loud as I could and play songs off my playlist on my phone felt absolutely amazing.

I'd forgotten the little things I was no longer able to enjoy until I had access again and let me tell you; they're not so little. They're huge. Don't ever take for granted the ability to have a radio in your car. To be able to take a drive and listen to music is so needed sometimes, I think, for us all.

I thought I was going to have a PTSD moment when I picked up the car if it tried to connect to anything, but Wayne made sure to get all of it hooked up so I would have full control over it because before, I had not been the one to connect anything. I was not the one controlling it. So that was really sweet and I'm so thankful. Thank you, Wayne, and thank God.

Ethicality

Innocent Until Proven Guilty

I recently came across a Facebook page I'd been avoiding for two years. Tonight I wanted to be nosey, in all honesty. And I've always encouraged people to write. Write their feelings. It's healing to do so. But this person, well, they write to preach their opinions onto others as if they're facts. Their way or the highway type thing. I'm not one to judge. To each their own. But do not write to preach. That's not healing for anyone, not even yourself. In fact, I felt less than healed or encouraged after reading the conflicting words that came from her mouth.

This person, in my eyes, is a felon. Not a convicted felon yet.. But here's the thing about that, it's the crime that was committed that I have a personal problem with. It was against me. It was felony wiretapping and stealing mail from my mailbox. Insurance fraud, money laundering. You name it... she did it to me. So why, after all this time, do I feel like I have to speak out? Well, it's simple. To tell my side of the story and to expose the truth about who she really is.

I saw this side of her in 2013. She violated an ethics law by accessing my personal information. She used her computer software at her job to find out everything she could about me. Then she repeated what she found to my husband, boyfriend at the time. If he hadn't begged me not to get her fired, well, maybe it would've saved many from enduring the BS she's brought to my life.

I pray for justice in my situation. She ruined me. Mentally, physically, financially and emotionally. I'm sure you're thinking, how can someone have that much power over another? Well, it's simple. Identity Theft and stalking.

41

Another Year Down

Yesterday was my 41st birthday. I was actually looking forward to this one. Why not? I'd removed myself from a toxic situation, and I have great friends and family. All I could see were the positive things for this year. My book release, my art, maybe some resolve in the identity theft.

I decided to have a small get-together at my house to celebrate. Just a few friends and my sister, nothing huge. It was fun. Leslie's husband made us some really nasty shots, but they were pretty. He mixed tequila with Sprite and cut up strawberries really tiny to top them off. We were tipsy and laughing at everything.

Leslie came early and decorated. I had balloons, banners and a backdrop for pics. I even had someone send me flowers. I'm still not sure who those were from. I know who they're not from, for sure!

That night I sent a text to a guy I'd been talking to. I'd invited him to come, but he never said yes or no. I felt avoided that day. The morning text was now an afternoon text with a simple "happy birthday 🎈".

I knew that he didn't want a relationship. He had life stuff he wanted to handle first. I respect that. He told me no expectations from him. I tried really hard not to have any...

When you get used to someone texting you every day, you kind of start expecting the text. Right? I mean, I did. I didn't even realize I was doing that. Is it normal? Like, I don't even know. My situation has caused me to question everything I do or say and I still apologize for everything.

Well, as the night went on and no text saying, hey, can't make it... I decided to send a text myself. I sent a simple F*** It. I received a paragraph back. It hurt my feelings. I immediately felt like I'd done something wrong because I'd expressed my feelings. I think it's ok to express your feelings, except I was and now I felt because I had, I lost him. I lost something I never had, to begin with, I guess. A situationship, if you will.

The letdown was respectful, considering I could've just been ghosted. I mean, that's happened to me. That shit stings. But, I found myself blaming ME for sending one text. I needed more of an explanation in regard to me. The need for validation is there. Daddy issues much? Probably. I never received validation from him.

My friends and I were on the back porch when I got the text and my mood changed instantly. Leslie noticed. I sent her a text so I wouldn't have to announce it and shared with her what happened. Lindsey, sitting next to me, could tell I was about to cry. She asked me to come inside with her.

We went to my bathroom and I told her what had happened. She grabbed me and hugged me and I let out a big cry. Why? Why was I crying over some guy that made it clear he didn't want me? Why didn't I get it through my head I was never going to be anything to him?

It's simple. I have feelings. My heart is huge. I don't open up to many people. There's very few that I feel safe enough to do that with. There's very few people that can understand me or my humor and when I find people that get me, I latch on. I want to be understood. I guess my point is I just want to be loved. That's all. I haven't been able to figure out and accept that it's okay for some people to just not like you.

I never dated anyone. Literally. This guy asked me to brunch and said it's not a date and my dumbass was like wow, I'm on my first date at 40. Everyone else just wanted to hang out with me. So

I think from the beginning, I was the problem. But here's what I know to be true. He laughed too. He opened up, too and those things made me feel like we felt the same about each other. I really liked him and felt there was a strong connection, but the level of effort I required and the level he could give didn't match.

I'm still trying to work out in my head if it's okay for someone to cut you off like that because you had an accidental or normal reaction/expectation. Or if I'm being ridiculous? I don't know. I know that it hurt my heart on my birthday and I now had a "heart hole," as my sister calls it.

We ended up going to a local bar shortly after my birthday cry and I just wasn't feeling it. I wanted to go home to my dogs. To my bed. Where I felt safe and comfortable. I still had more tears that needed to fall.

When I got home, I let them fall. I didn't cry as long as I thought I would. I think I was just emotionally exhausted and my heart and mind just wanted rest.

Summer didn't show up. She has things in her life going on. Who doesn't? Everyone I know is going through something, but we show up for each other. That's what we do. She has been coming over every night for the past few weeks for me to listen to her problems and I do. But again, when I need her to show up for me, she's not there. Love them from a distance, I guess.

Two birthdays in a row, two different guys, two different heartbreaks. But I had cake and people that love me.

Here's to 41 and figuring it out.

Erased

I guess I'm just
A season
You erased me
With no reason

I was only there
A short time
To fill a void
You were never mine

I don't know how
I got it wrong
To to actually think
I could belong

I'll just fade away
It's over now
Maybe some other day
You'll come around

I'll miss our talks
And the time we had
It couldn't have been
All that bad

I'd like to think
Maybe we were right
Just the wrong time
And I'd be hard
To leave behind

I feel erased
As if I didn't matter
You just vanished
My light's now scattered

I just wanted closure
To understand why
We couldn't start over

You matched my wit
It was a good fit
You made me smile
When it had been a while

It was last September
The heart
Always remembers

I'll be okay
I've survived worse
My heart has holes
But I'll fix it first

No expectations
Is what you said
But then you went
And got inside my head

I found myself
Looking forward to texts
Just a good a morning
You were always charming

I'll be healed
If you ever come back
Maybe you'll do the same
And they're be nothing we lack

Moving Forward

I can't help but wonder if anyone out there can make sense of this. What's the motive? Money? Affairs? Other activities? The goal of writing the book was for me to be able to make sense of it. To go back through all my files and maybe something would stand out. Maybe I'd missed something.

That hasn't happened yet. I know the how and the who, but not the why or even all the what's.

All I know is the toll it took on me, the privacy that I lost, friends, money, job and health. I still have no resolution in the case. I'm hoping with this book I can help others approach their situation differently so that they can achieve a better outcome than me.

Check your emails. Check the trash folders. Stop sharing your iCloud account. Change your passwords frequently. Use different emails for business, pleasure and social media.

Know that the people closest to you can hurt you, but you can survive it. People will show up for you if even if they only have a listening ear to offer. People will leave you because they don't understand and that's ok. You'll be ok.

I continue to sit on the back porch. It's just something I haven't been able to stop. I have a hard time being inside my home to this day. I still can't watch tv.

Even though I've moved and removed myself, the effects it's had on me remain. I'm still waiting on unemployment. It's been eight months and nothing. I'm currently seeking work so that I can have health insurance and an income. Maybe I'll be able to go back to the doctor and get to the bottom of it.

The pain and suffering caused by others will likely remain forever. It's how I chose to cope, I believe, that's helped me be okay at least enough to continue getting up every morning and doing "the things," painting and sitting in silence.

I pray for justice in my situation. The money is gone. I doubt I'll ever recover that, but I hope for justice in a different way. I hope that one day I'll stand in a courtroom and be able to tell my story and have the court of law recognize all that's happened to me.

I want the world to know. I want the ex-wife to be charged in her role. This changed my life! It took everything I had away from me. The pain and suffering I've endured were unbelievable and unnecessary. It affected everyone around me. My friends and family would start having the same paranoia I did about devices. And honestly, everyone should because it happens all the time. People just don't know what to look for.

I hope this book has been educational. I want to protect everyone I can from people like the ones that assisted in my situation. I want people to understand that emotional abuse and trauma are not okay and to seek therapy and talk. Talking was key for me. The conversations I'd had with friends and family and being heard helped me tremendously. I didn't fall apart. I survived.

I don't know if I'll ever make sense of my situation, but my goal is to help others recognize the signs of identity theft and abuse. It doesn't always have to be physical. Emotional abuse, to me, is more harmful. I'm still learning to rebuild my confidence and remember who I was, but I'm liking the new Brooke. The new Brooke is stronger. She's changed, but she's better. She's a survivor!

October 2022 Writing in my do-it-yourself memoir

December 2022, watching the sunset

October 2022, watching the sunset

December 31, 2022, Toasting to the new year

Acknowledgment

Words cannot express my gratitude to my sisters Audra and Lisa and my mom for helping me make decisions on the book itself. My deepest thanks to Leslie and Audra for reading my book prior to submission and giving words of encouragement along the way. Thank you to Lindsey who encouraged me to tell my story and felt as passionate as me. I could not have undertaken this journey without you all.

About the Author

I'm Brooke. I am a victim of identity theft by someone I know. I was diagnosed with PTSD from my experience. I've survived my situation, but I am still coping with the aftermath of what it's done to me mentally, physically, and emotionally.

Made in United States
Orlando, FL
27 May 2023